From the Sanctuary
to the Streets

Insights and Adventures in Power Evangelism

Charles Bello and Brian Blount

Dedicated to our fathers and mothers in the faith who paved the way for us, our friends and co-workers in the kingdom, and those we have the privilege of pouring our lives into.

Praise for *From the Sanctuary to the Streets*

You can read this book for the stories and have a wonderful time, sometimes laughing and sometimes crying, or you can read this book for its down-to-earth practical combination of classical Christian spirituality and (literally) hands-on evangelism based on an understanding of the New Testament that (strangely) expects it to work. The stories then become encouragement and examples to go and do likewise. I recommend the latter type of reading; but if you do the other type, do not be surprised if you get drawn in to the teaching. A delightful, practical book I am happy to recommend.

Dr. Peter H. Davids
Professor of Biblical Theology at St. Stephen's University
Author of *A Commentary on the Epistle of James, The First Epistle of Peter,* and *2 Peter and Jude*

From the Sanctuary to the Streets is a great resource and "must read" for everyone—individuals and churches—who are interested in engaging in power evangelism. The authors emphasize not only what God wants to do through us, but also the work He is doing in us, as we step out in faith to partner with Him in His mission and ministry. Weaving Scripture, story and insights gleaned from personal experience, the authors present a compelling account of how we, as followers of Jesus, can walk in both His words and works in our everyday lives. *From the Sanctuary to the Streets* will challenge you to take the ministry of Jesus with you wherever you go.

Jack Moraine
Sr. Pastor of Vineyard Community Church, Gilbert, AZ
Author of *Healing Ministry: A Training Manual for Believers*

There has been a great deal of interest in "outreach, prophetic evangelism, treasure hunts" and whatever else is an appropriate way to describe evangelism. What there hasn't been is this thorough study on the entire spectrum. I love Brian's revivalist heart and Charles' compassion and teaching gift. Together they have given us inspiration and a good body of practice for how to move out of the church into our world with good news and a demonstration of the kingdom's power. This is a fun read and very practical. I could see this as required reading for some of the many emerging schools and for those who just need a little push to get out there share the love of Christ.

Denny Cline
Senior Leader, Jesus Pursuit Church

Charles and Brian have been working with the Vineyard churches in Europe for more than a decade, teaching ordinary people how to minister in the power of the Holy Spirit. This is a thrilling book built on truth and experience. It is a good mix of honesty and encouragement as Charles and Brian attempt to walk in that place of hearing the call to discipleship and doing the ministry modeled by Jesus in the Gospels.

Martin Buehlman
Church planter
National Director of Vineyard Churches in Germany, Austria, and Switzerland

We have known Charles and Brian for many years. They are not only anointed to *do* power ministry, but they are specially gifted to equip us average Christians to do the ministry of Jesus. Their down-to-earth, and very practical, teaching has helped prepare hundreds of our missionaries to prophesy, heal the sick, and drive out demons. We especially love their honesty about the natural questions that arise as we so often experience the "now, but the not yet" of the kingdom of God. Their personal stories will inspire you and give you faith to take the RISK and step out to see what God will do through you!

John and Jamie Zumwalt
Authors of *Passion for the Heart of God* and *Simple Obsession*
Founders of Heart of God Ministries missionary training agency

I believe that this book represents a call to all churches. The church is facing challenging times and, more than anything else, we need to hear the words of Jesus showing us how to navigate through these challenges. I believe the title of this book represents what Jesus is saying to the church today. In an honest and open way, Charles and Brian share their journey and what they have learned as they responded to Jesus' call. Their stories are an invitation to all of us to embark on this journey ourselves. Learning from their practical wisdom will help us all. I felt inspired and challenged by their stories.

Dr. Richard Clinton
Senior Pastor, The Springs Vineyard
Co-author of *Unlocking Your Giftedness* and *Starting Well*

Acknowledgments

In practicing a lifestyle of healing and power evangelism and in the course of writing this book, we have gleaned from many who paved the way before us in power ministry, such as John Wimber and Blaine Cook. Foremost, we have been shaped and influenced by the ministry of John Wimber. His life and ministry continues to have a profound impact on what we do. In the spirit of 2 Timothy 2:2, "The things you have heard me say in the presence of many witnesses entrust to reliable men who will also be qualified to teach others," his wisdom pours through the pages of this book.

Much appreciation is given to Brian's wife, Jeanine Blount. Jeanine took Brian's wonderful stories and insights and together they put them in written form. Then she took Charles' written stories, commentaries, and insights and wove them together with Brian's material to help us create a single coherent book.

Special thanks to our friends Jack Moraine, Laura Bauer, Kelly Arndt, and Sally Hanan for proof reading our manuscript; and for Dr. Peter Davids, Pastor Jack Moraine and Pastor Robert Gilbert for reading over our manuscript with a theologian's perspective. Their input was invaluable, and we carefully weighed all their suggestions.

As always, the time and energy it takes to write a book means that our families must pay a price. Charles thanks his wife Dianna for her continual love and encouragement. Brian thanks Jeanine, their six children (Annalisa, Tyler, Amberlyn, Josiah, Nathaniel, and Ashley), as well as Jeanine's parents, Jack and Bonnie Spratt, whose frequent help with the grandchildren has freed up the time for Brian and Jeanine to complete this work.

Authors' Note

Because this book is written by two authors and much of the book involves accounts of our personal adventures, we acknowledge the challenge of helping the reader understand which of us is narrating the book at any point. To clarify this, let us note that all instructional or non-storytelling aspects of the book are written as a collaborative effort. When moving from teaching aspects of the book to a story or personal account, we will clarify the individual narrating by putting their name in parenthesis, such as (Charles) or (Brian). Once that personal account is over, the authorship is once again collaborative.

Table of Contents

Jesus' Job Description

Upon returning from forty days in the barren wilderness after His baptism, Jesus was a changed man. Impassioned with His heavenly Father's love, empowered by the Holy Spirit's strength, tried and tested by temptation, Jesus was now a man on a mission. Returning to His home town of Nazareth on the Sabbath, as was His custom, Jesus found Himself at the local synagogue. He was asked to read and was handed the scroll of Isaiah. Unrolling it, He found the place He was looking for and read the following:

> *The Spirit of the Lord is on me, because he has anointed me to preach good news to the poor. He has sent me to proclaim freedom for the prisoners and recovery of sight for the blind, to release the oppressed, to proclaim the year of the Lord's favor. (Luke 4:18-19)*

Reading the passage, Jesus began to explain to all those listening that this scripture at this very moment was being fulfilled in their midst. In contemporary language, Jesus laid out His job description. To paraphrase, He said, "This is why the Father sent me and the Holy Spirit has empowered me. I am to preach and demonstrate the good news of the in-breaking of God's kingdom to the poor, the marginalized, the oppressed, and the powerless. This is not just some future event; it is happening right now through my ministry."

Fast Forward to 1984

Twenty-six years ago, I (Charles), as a young pastor doing my morning devotionals, read Luke 4:18-19. As I pondered these words, I heard the still small voice of God whisper on the inside of me, *"This is your job description."* And with that whispered nudge came an understanding that as Jesus' disciple, I was called to the same ministry and activity as Jesus.

My first response back to God was, "No! That was Jesus' job description." At that time I could not even begin to imagine myself healing the sick and driving out demons. I convinced myself that the words I thought I heard from God were simply the result of an overactive imagination. The conversation ended, but in the weeks and months that followed, unrest began to stir within as God began to challenge my paradigm of what it meant to follow Jesus.

I was raised Catholic, the oldest son of an Air Force enlisted man who loved his wife and family. Other than moving to a new airbase every few years, my upbringing was normal and uneventful. As a conscientious Catholic, I had confidence that miracles were done by Jesus, His immediate disciples and by the saints throughout the centuries. As an evangelical pastor, I even held out hope and belief that these same kinds of things could possibly happen today through special men and women who were anointed by God. I just knew that I was not one of those special anointed individuals; besides, most of those I had observed doing "power ministry" seemed to be overenthusiastic showmen who excelled in exaggeration and emotionalism.

I had come to know God in a personal way during the Jesus movement of the late 60's and early 70's. My early adult Christian formation was shaped by the Catholic Charismatic movement and later by the Shepherding or Discipleship Movement. This movement initially emphasized personal accountability, character development, and transparent relationships among church members and leaders. In time, this movement gained a reputation for controlling and abusive behavior with a great deal of emphasis placed on obedience to one's own pastor. What initially helped shape my character and ministry for the good began to be manipulative, authoritarian, and theologically unsound. As a young pastor and father in my late twenties, I was now ready for an expression of Christianity a little more subdued, balanced and mainstream, so I started my seminary education at a Baptist university.

In the months following my truncated conversation with God about my job description, a river of repentance began to form from within. I began to suspect that I had let myself become lukewarm. During a conversation with a fellow pastor, I was asked if I had heard of a signs and wonders conference by a minister named John Wimber, the founder of the Vineyard movement. An explosion of faith rose up from within as well as a rushing conviction that I was to attend this conference. Months later, I was in a large auditorium in Anaheim, California listening to a self-effacing middle-aged musician turned pastor read from Luke 4:18-19. I remember John pointing his finger toward the crowd and saying, "This is your job description." His words were followed by demonstrations of healing. What I had heard God whisper in my heart was now being proclaimed from a stage: that Jesus' job-description was to be my job description. I repented of my lack of faith and I took up the challenge to follow Christ whatever the cost.

I began attending equipping conferences and workshops and then I would practice on the people in my congregation. Like my feeble efforts at personal evangelism, my newfound healing ministry was met with both success and failure. In the decades to follow I experienced the joy of seeing cancer healed, deaf ears opened and hundreds of people coming to Christ as a response to experiencing His power. I also had more questions than answers as to why hundreds of people I prayed for failed to get better. One of the more perplexing incidents took place one Sunday when two women came forward for prayer. They both had cancer. One was a dear single woman in her forties who had dedicated her whole life to the Lord, serving as a missionary in South Africa. The second woman was a soon to be grandmother in her fifties. The second woman was healed, and months later, I sat praying with the missionary at her hospital bed as she breathed her last breath.

Despite the trepidation stemming from my unanswered questions about why God healed some people and not others, the weight of Scripture and the conviction of the Holy Spirit gave me courage to continue praying for the sick. I found the confidence to move forward through the help of credible ministers and simple ministry models rooted in compassion and dependence on the empowering presence of the Holy Spirit.

Fast Forward to 1995

As for us we cannot help speaking about what we have seen and heard. (Acts 4:20)

My (Brian's) journey in power evangelism has led me to say the same thing Peter and John said before the Sanhedrin: "I cannot help speaking about what I have seen and heard." My biggest prayer is that the same fire gets into your heart: that you cannot help speaking about what you've seen and heard as you enter into your own power evangelism experiences.

I came to know Jesus in a personal way at sixteen. Up to that time my life was heading nowhere. I grew up in a broken home—my dad left my mom when I was a toddler, and I spent a lot of my childhood being shuffled around between grandparents and friends. My mother worked hard to support herself and her two young children, all the while battling depression and her own pain. She really did her best, and I know she loved me.

I started drinking, huffing gasoline, and smoking pot by age eleven. During my adolescent years I dropped out of school, became sexually active, and was in and out of boys' homes and rehab centers, always trying to fill the painful void of not having a father who loved me enough to stick around. My home life was unstable and full of pain.

At sixteen, a friend of the family who was a father figure in my life invited me to a weekend Christian retreat. I didn't want to go, but out of respect for him, I went. That weekend I heard the gospel and encountered Jesus. I was immediately delivered from any interest in drugs as my emptiness was filled with God's love. I discovered a sense of purpose for the first time in my life. I felt welcomed into a loving community of new friends and older men and women who became spiritual fathers and mothers to me and helped me grow in my new-found faith.

In the years that followed, my faith was shaped through a number of para-church organizations and youth camps until everything came full circle and I began serving as a camp counselor myself. During these years, I was introduced to the Holy Spirit and His power. I knew the power of God had radically changed my life, but I had never really seen the Holy Spirit move through me in a powerful way.

A year before meeting Charles, I had an encounter with the Holy Spirit that forever changed the course of my life and sent me on a journey to pursue more of Jesus, His mission, and the power of God. It was my first experience with power evangelism, which is simply people giving their lives to the Lord in response to a demonstration of His power.

It was the summer of 1995. I had been invited to be a camp counselor for a district denominational youth camp along with some friends of mine: David Mullikin and Jon Havens. We were really excited to share our lives with the campers and see what God would do. About a week before the camp started, I had an unusual experience. I woke up from a deep sleep, sobbing with tears rolling down my face as I felt a heavy burden I couldn't explain. When I was able to pray intelligibly, these words came out of my mouth repeatedly: "Oh that the love of God would come upon the camp!" I had never had an experience like this, so I was a little shaken, yet excited to see what God would do.

It was customary to arrive at the camp a day before so we could connect with the other counselors and discuss the plans and strategy for the camp. After reading over the camp itinerary for the coming week, Jon, David, and I realized that there were no spiritual activities planned—no Bible studies, no devotionals, and no prayer meetings. There were to be evening worship services, but experience had taught us that these tended to be camp songs followed by pep talks with little spiritual content. At that point, my friends and I weren't sure what we had signed up for, so we asked if we could add a class of our own. We called it "The Cross and the Flame." We didn't really know what we were going to do other than share our testimonies and talk about Jesus and the little we knew about the Holy Spirit.

The next day, a couple hundred kids arrived at the camp grounds, and out of that group we had six teenage campers show up for our elective workshop. Though the numbers were small, the kids seemed to engage with our stories. That evening we had our evening worship service. Jon was leading worship, though he had been strongly instructed not to play anything slow-paced in fear that it would breed an emotional frenzy. After hearing the sermon, I couldn't tell if we were being instructed to follow Jesus, Buddha, or some other golden path. I'm not trying to be sarcastic—it really was quite a liberal camp.

During the service, the campers were allowed to share short "popcorn" prayers, where someone pops up and shares their prayer... it's a weird youth camp thing. You could tell the popcorn prayer time became uncomfortable to the camp leaders as strange prayers started popping out of the campers' mouths: "Lord we ask that your kingdom would come," and "Show us your power," and "Let us encounter your love." The plan was to end the service around a bonfire with Jon playing his guitar... but not too slowly.

Out of nowhere, it seemed, youth began to raise their hands and enter into worship. The atmosphere appeared to be charged with the manifest presence of God; there was electricity in the air as a hunger, tenderness, and brokenness filled the kids. I remember I was shocked but excited to see what was happening. Although Jon is a great worship leader, he was so constrained in what he was allowed to do that there didn't seem to be any correlation between what he was playing and the level of worship the youth were entering into. Despite Jon's best effort to comply with the leaders' instructions, the camp clergy became very nervous and started shouting, "It's time to stop and eat smores!!" As you can imagine, it was a very awkward moment.

The next thing I knew, there was a small seventh-grade boy tugging at my shirt saying, "Brian, I have a question for you. How come when the Holy Spirit comes, these pastors and leaders tell Him to go away?" My mouth dropped open, dumbfounded by the question, and unsure how to answer. This young man had more spiritual sensitivity than the trained professionals.

Before I could answer his question, a young girl came up yelling, "There's something wrong! There's something wrong! A girl fell on the ground and there's something wrong with her!" I didn't know what to think. Had someone tripped? A heat stroke? A seizure? David, myself, and the seventh-grade boy ran over to find out what was going on. We saw a young girl, about sixteen, shaking uncontrollably on the ground and speaking in tongues. I remember looking at David and saying, "We have two choices: we can walk away, or we can see what God is doing and get into a lot of trouble." We chose trouble.

I asked the young girl, "What is God saying to you?" but all she could do was speak in tongues and shake.

After asking her a third time, she got up and said, "God wants to come and touch people with His love." I was shocked because this was the same thing I had heard in my prayers a week before, and I had been shaking and speaking in tongues just like her. Then the girl touched another girl, and when she did the other girl fell to the ground and lay there motionless.

At this point, kids from everywhere starting coming to us, confessing their sins, giving their lives to Jesus, and shaking and falling to the ground. David, Jon, and I were overwhelmed, so we recruited the six kids who had been in our Bible study to pray for people. During this excitement, I felt a tap on my shoulder. I turned around and saw a young man standing behind me. His name was J.P. I had known J.P. for a couple of years and had seen him at other youth camps. He reminded me of my former self— he was always on the fringe. I had always wondered why he was at these church camps. J.P. said, "Brian, what in the hell is going on here?!"

I replied, "J.P., this is Jesus and the power of the Holy Spirit."

Then the young girl who had started this whole thing said, "Oh J.P., God loves you!" She hugged him and began to pray over him. Later, J.P. told me she was praying things no one but

God could have known. He was so overwhelmed that he fell to the ground weeping. As the girl continued to pray, she unexpectedly said, "I command this demonic thing to come off of you and leave." Keep in mind, this was all new to these kids and to us for that matter. I was kneeling over J.P. as this was spoken and could literally feel a cold, dark presence leave him.

I asked J.P. if he had ever been saved. He said, "Saved? What the *&@#%^* are you talking about?" I repeated the question and he cried out, "Jesus, please save me!"

More and more youth were being drawn to what was happening with J.P. and the others. They came over out of curiosity but then had similar experiences with the Holy Spirit. I looked up at one point and saw the clergy, leaders, and camp staff literally hiding behind trees and benches with looks of horror on their faces.

Before long, one of the clergy had had enough. He was screaming at us to stop this nonsense and demanded that the kids get off the ground and head to their cabins. But they couldn't—they were completely unable to get up having been overtaken by the power of the Holy Spirit. This infuriated him even more. He picked up one of the girls by the leg and began to drag her, telling her to get up as she lay there as if in a trance. It was both comical and scary—part of me wondered whether God would fry this man on the spot for his insolence! Then I heard my name, David's name, and Jon's name being called by the dean clergyman of the camp. "Get into my office now!"

I said, "I'll be right there, but let me grab my Bible."

This enraged the dean as he blurted out, "You don't need your Bible!"

For the next couple hours, we were scolded by the pastors. Some blamed us for causing this "emotionalism" and nonsense. Others scolded us for bringing a Pentecostal spirit into the camp. Others said this was demonic. My response was "It wasn't my fault!" Like any bold man of faith, I blamed the girl. "It was her fault!"

The camp dean clergyman said, "Do you know what will happen to me when my district superintendent finds out about this?"

I'm not condoning my response, but this is what I said: "If you don't have the balls to stand up to your district superintendent and understand that what happened here tonight was God, then you have a bigger problem on your hands." Needless to say, my response didn't go over too well. I was a twenty year old, full of passion, but not a lot of tact; but to tell the truth, I don't know if I would have done it any differently, looking back on it now.

That next day, our class attendance was so great that we could barely fit everyone in the meeting hall. Despite the salvations and wonderful things that happened the night before, I continued to carry the brunt of the persecution from the clergy. I remember being in the dean's cabin again, by myself, with eight to ten staff and clergy as they continued to chastise me. There were tears and people were visibly upset about how I had ruined their camp. Again, my bold response was, "I didn't do anything! I told you it was that girl. I just participated in what God was doing." This upset them even more.

One of the clergymen said, "These kids are going around speaking in tongues and talking about these experiences. This is bringing nothing but confusion. You've ruined our camp!"

I have to admit, I was extremely intimidated. Here I was, just a young Christian leader with little experience at the time, and I didn't have the theological understanding or ability to explain what had happened. All I could say was, "The only way this will continue to cause confusion and misunderstanding is if you don't do your jobs as clergy and open up Scripture to explain to them what has happened." Needless to say, that didn't go over very well either.

However, even while this was happening, God was continuing to move. As I was taking one for the team, Jon and David were with the youth in the sanctuary. Kids had approached them wanting to experience what others had the night before. Knowing that they weren't allowed to pray with the kids in the sanctuary, they snuck off to secluded areas of the camp and prayed for them there. Kids were coming to Jesus, shaking and falling to the ground as the power of the Holy Spirit came upon them. That week changed my life forever, as well as the lives of many of those youth. In fact, I occasionally keep in contact with J.P. He is now a pastor.

This was my first encounter with an in-breaking of the kingdom of God. I thought to myself that if God could come into a place where even the clergy didn't welcome Him, then how much more could He come upon people who are hungry for Him and who welcome His presence? If the lost could be powerfully saved in a place where the Holy Spirit was not given permission to move, how much more could happen out on the streets with disciples who carried a passion for the presence and power of the Holy Spirit?

I began looking for a place where I could grow in my understanding of the Holy Spirit without having to fit into a hyper-spiritual, overly-charismatic mold. I had a hunger and desire to see evangelism happen, and I also had a deep passion for healing ministry. Up to this point, however, the only people I had seen move in the power of the Holy Spirit did it in ways that seemed unnatural to me, and I had no desire to emulate their models of ministry.

In 1996, I attended a Vineyard conference, and for the first time in my life, I saw ministry happening not from the man on the stage, but by ordinary people in the congregation. Miraculous things were happening in a totally non-hyped "normal" atmosphere. I was overcome with the sense that this was what I had been looking for. This was the type of ministry that I could relate to—normal people being used by God in amazing ways and doing it in a way that was naturally supernatural.

Upon returning home from the conference, my girlfriend (now my wife), Jeanine, and I started looking for a Vineyard church in our city. I wanted to get around people who ministered in the same way I saw at the conference. Charles Bello was the pastor of the Oklahoma City Vineyard and we immediately connected with each other. Jeanine and I arrived at a time when the church was in a huge transition, and I think we were an answer to their prayers as much as they were to ours. Over the following months, I began watching Charles closely and learning everything I could from him.

We attended classes he taught on healing ministry, and we followed him around every chance we got. I'm sure he sometimes got tired of all my phone calls and visits; but for the first time in my life, I felt like I had found a model for ministry I could embrace that actually worked, and I was zealous to learn more.

Run, Forrest, Run!

By the mid to late 90's, Charles and I were doing equipping seminars and leading teams in North America, Asia, and Western Europe. We were primarily instructing people in power ministry: prophetic ministry, healing, and deliverance. In 2004, we were asked by a German Vineyard pastor and dear friend, Reinhard Rehberg, to help him lead a team of Germans and Swiss on a short term mission trip to Romania.

We settled on a plan to experiment with a different format and conduct a "mobile school of power evangelism" which would equip both the mission team and the Romanian churches we were working with. Instead of simply doing seminars in the churches, we decided to do equipping workshops in the mornings throughout the week and then couple the German and Swiss participants with the Romanian church members in the afternoons to practice what they learned. Our curriculum involved teaching about the kingdom of God, praying for the sick, and sharing prophetic insight with strangers.

On one of our first days in Iasi, Romania after a morning of teaching on kingdom ministry, we took the teams out in public to practice what we'd learned in private. Some of the teams made their way to the local hospital; other teams went to the shopping mall, the downtown area, and the outlying gypsy villages. I took my team to one of the many local parks.

Our approach was fairly simple and straightforward: we looked around and if anyone caught our interest, we asked God to give us insight into something in their lives that He would like us to speak into or something He would want us to share with them. Then we politely and prayerfully moved toward that person to share the insight we'd received. Sometimes we would simply frame our conversation with this: "We are followers of

Jesus, and we are trying to learn how to hear God's voice, and this is what we think we are hearing from God for you..." Then those we were speaking with would have the opportunity to tell us if we were on the right track or not. More times than not, this led to some very interesting conversations about God. Other times we simply approached people, introduced ourselves as Christians, and asked if there was anything we could pray for. If it was obvious that they were sick, we asked if we could pray for healing. Whenever anyone accepted our request for prayer, we always asked that God pour out His love and affection at that moment.

On this particular day, we were not having much success. Our prophetic insight seemed to be off the mark. Either we were mistaken in what we believed God was saying or we were not being very effective in sharing in a way that would invite conversation. As one failure followed another, I found myself getting increasingly frustrated. It is one thing to fail in front of strangers, but to fail in the midst of the very people I was training was almost too much to bear. I found my mind was growing dark with thoughts such as, *"What are you doing here? This really sucks. You need to go back to the United States. This is a waste of time."* I was ready to call it quits and give up for the day. It is not unusual for negative thoughts such as these to bombard our minds, trying to distract us from pressing into God and believing that His kingdom will come.

During this thought process, I saw an older couple with a younger lady in a park, sitting down by a tree. We had about twenty minutes before we had to get back to the church for dinner, so I said, "Guys, let's try this one more time. Let's go over to that family over there."

Everyone agreed and we walked to them. As we were walking up, I experienced a sharp pain shoot up my left side. I had learned that these kinds of sympathetic pains are sometimes indications of God's desire to heal. Through one of the interpreters, I asked the family if any of them had a pain in their left side. The young girl indicated that she did, so we explained that we were followers of Jesus and sometimes God reveals things to us for other people. We believed God had showed us the pain because He wanted to heal her. We asked if we could pray for her and she said yes.

As we prayed, the presence of God came upon her body and the pain completely left. We explained the gospel to her and in the ensuing conversation she surrendered her life to Jesus. She then introduced us to the others with her: her mom and dad. The three of them had been kicked out of their home, and they were living in the park. She told us her dad was very ill, but we couldn't understand the nature of his illness. He was very weak and shaking, very sickly looking and he seemed to have Parkinson's disease. Being filled with compassion for this man, I asked for permission to pray for him.

Initially, the man didn't want anything to do with us, even though his daughter had just been healed and given her life to the Lord. He didn't want to engage in any kind of conversation. I kept persisting and smiling, trying to talk with him. I even tried giving him and his wife American candies I had in my pocket. I was trying everything—even bribery with candy! Finally, he agreed to let me pray for him.

I asked him to stand. As soon as he did, he immediately fell to the ground. It wasn't because of any great power being released. It was because this man was so sick that he couldn't even stand for more than a few seconds, so I kneeled down next to him and, through the interpreter, I asked what was going on in his body. He said from the waist down he couldn't feel anything and from the waist up he was in pain. We began to pray and ask that God would release His healing presence.

After a few short moments of praying, he began to weep. He said he felt blood flowing through his legs. The numbness was leaving his legs, and the pain was also leaving. I said, "Do something you couldn't do before."

The man stood up, and all the trembling he'd had before had completely stopped, and his countenance changed. He was standing strong. Again, I repeated my instruction. I said, "Do something more that you couldn't do before!"

He began to run in place. Then, his pace quickened and he took off in a sprint. He ran around the park, even running up and down a large flight of stairs. After he circled the park, he returned to us panting.

He told us he was sixty-seven years old. I said, "I'm thirty, and I don't think I could do what you just did!" We led the man to Christ while the rest of the team prayed for his wife who was deaf in one ear. Her hearing returned as a result of their prayers.

After we led the man to Christ, he immediately took off in a run. He kept running and running and running. It was such a powerful encounter, and we had almost given up because we hadn't seen any progress. I am so thankful we didn't throw in the towel in our discouragement. We saw three salvations, a deaf ear opened, a pain in the left side healed, and a very sick man healed by the power of God and running all over the place. Not a bad deal for a couple hours in the park!

When we got back to the church that evening, we began to share testimonies of what happened. Several of the Romanians who were with us kept saying, "Today we saw a real miracle." They were smiling from ear to ear.

The next day, some of the team went back to check on the family. They saw the daughter and the mother in the park. The team members asked where the father was. They said, "Ever since you prayed for him, all he does is run and run and run." It was like the man had turned into Forrest Gump—he just kept running and running and running!

That week in Romania was full of similar stories. Many, but not all, that we prayed for experienced some kind of tangible presence of peace or love, and at times others would begin to visibly shake or tremble. There were many instances when people were healed from their physical conditions, including deaf ears, blind eyes, and tumors. We would always follow the demonstrations of the love and power of God with a simple presentation of the Gospel. In that one week in Romania we saw around one hundred people surrender their lives to God, mostly through the prayers of newly-trained German, Swiss and Romanian disciples. We found it much easier to explain the truth of the gospel with people who had just experienced the loving presence of God. Proclamation and demonstration are a powerful combination.

In every country or city we go to, we hear a similar complaint: it is really hard to do ministry in my country. From the Germans we hear, "Germany is really hard to reach." From the Swiss we hear, "Swiss people are not open to the Gospel," In Romania we hear, "It's really tough to reach the Romanian people." In the United States we hear similar complaints about the sophisticated northeast, the fundamentalist Bible Belt, the hedonist west coast. One begins to wonder who is telling the church this. Is this the Spirit of God, or is this the enemy?

Because of what Christ has done through His death and resurrection, there is no closed nation, region, or neighborhood. Every nation is open to the gospel. There may be suffering and persecution involved, and at times it may cost some of us our lives, but there is no such thing as a closed nation. The Holy Spirit is in the world, drawing mankind to its savior. The Spirit empowered message of the nearness of the kingdom of God still works. We often find it easier to believe that God can move in impoverished, third world nations, but the truth of the matter is that the kingdom of God is at hand in our own country.

It's amazing what we have seen overseas, but we have seen even more healings and miracles here in the United States. We also continue to take newly trained disciples to bus stations, Walmarts, neighborhoods, and hospitals here. We always come with this same message: God loves you and He is near. We pray for the sick, and share whatever God gives us at the moment. Sometimes God releases a gift of healing, other times it might be prophetic insight. Still other times we are called to do the most difficult ministry and that is to mourn with those who mourn and comfort the suffering. Ministry, whether it's raising the dead or burying them, is always to be an expression of the compassionate love of Christ.

To understand empowered evangelism, we must first of all understand Jesus' approach to ministry. As His disciples, we are to take our cues from Him. The Gospels give us an account of the life and earthly ministry of Jesus, and as such they also provide a template for our service to God and to others.

Jesus' Job Description Is Our Job Description

If we are Jesus' disciples, then He is calling us to do what He did. Jesus' job description is our job description. If Jesus had been a mechanic, then we would be writing a book about being a good mechanic. If Jesus had been a farmer, then we would be teaching classes on how to be better farmers. Jesus went about healing the sick, freeing the oppressed, and declaring that the kingdom of God was at hand. God has given us the same ministry. We have been invited to participate in the ministry of Christ. What a privilege! What an honor it is to not only follow our Lord and listen to His words, but to actually do the things He did.

Jesus' job description was "The Spirit of the Lord is upon me for a reason: He has sent me to preach good news to the poor, proclaim freedom for the prisoners and recovery of sight for the blind" (Luke 4:18-19). When Jesus came on the scene He was declaring war. What was good news for the poor was bad news for the institutions and spirits that were keeping people in poverty. What was good news for the prisoners was bad news for the unrighteous and religious systems that were keeping people in bondage. It was good news for one group of people, but bad news for another. When we step into this job description that Jesus has called us to, we are stepping into a war and conflict.

There are many effective techniques and models for evangelism. Power evangelism is a term coined by John Wimber which refers to leading people into deeper relationship with Christ in response to an encounter with the power of God, such as through a healing or a prophetic word. It is a spontaneous, Spirit-inspired and Spirit-empowered presentation of the gospel.[1]

People are much more likely to come to Christ once they have had an experience with His love and power. The love of God demonstrated in a tangible, supernatural way breaks through the barriers people tend to put up against religion and Christianity. It bypasses their objections by providing an experience of the presence of the God who is inviting them into relationship with Himself.

We are both passionate equippers by gifting and conviction. In this book we share this fundamental belief: our lives with Christ must flow from the sanctuary into the streets. Sanctuary is a metaphor for intimacy with God. The streets are a metaphor for the mission of the gospel in the world. The purpose of this book is not so much to offer another technique as much as to share insights we have learned as we have stumbled our way through our journeys, and to share some of the adventures we have encountered along the way. This book is filled with our stories and those of others who have pressed into the secret place of intimacy and then outward into the mission of Christ among the un-churched. Through our trials, errors, successes, and failures we hope the insights we have gleaned will help you in your pursuit to live a life of intimacy with Christ and to have a Spirit-empowered ministry.

From the Sanctuary to the Streets

Living from the Sanctuary

Jesus was back in His hometown of Capernaum. News about His healing ministry was beginning to spread throughout the region. He was drawing large crowds from Decapolis, Jerusalem, Judea, and the provinces across the Jordan. He was teaching in the synagogues, healing the sick along the dusty roadways, driving out demons, and preaching the good news that the kingdom of God was at hand. The hometown crowd was left amazed and wondering out loud. "Where did Jesus get this kind of spiritual power?"

Mark 1:29-39 tells us Jesus made His way to the home of Simon (Peter) and Andrew. Simon and Andrew were among the earliest disciples of Jesus. Upon arriving there, He discovered the whole town gathering at Simon's front door. Well into the evening, the people lined up, waiting to be healed or delivered from afflicting spirits.

Very early the next morning while it was still dark and people were still asleep, Jesus quietly slipped out of Simon's house. He made His way out of the town to a secluded and solitary place. Listening to His heavenly Father, He got His marching orders for the day (and weeks) ahead.

This pattern of intense activity followed by solitude and quietness became a regular pattern in the life of Jesus. He seamlessly moved in and out of ministry activity. Jesus taught and served others out of a calm center of rest and inner peace. What He received in this quiet place was strong enough to resist the expectations of friends and family. This kind of inner resolve was only found in the loving presence of God. Jesus' example demonstrates that sustainable public ministry is grounded in personal private prayer.

While Jesus was praying in this secluded location, a crowd was beginning to gather in front of Simon's door. They all wanted something from Jesus, the miracle worker. Simon, to his horror, discovered that Jesus was no longer sleeping in His quarters, so Simon and his companions set out frantically looking for Jesus and the townspeople joined the manhunt as well. A little exasperated, Simon and the rest of the disciples found Jesus first. They excitedly explained to Him the seriousness of the situation. Jesus, unmoved by their expectation, simply told them, "Let us go somewhere else—to the nearby villages—so I can preach there also. That is why I have come" (Mark 1:38). Jesus was able to resist the wishes of the crowd and the expectation of His friends because He had taken the time and effort to hear God in the quietness of a secluded place.

We like to call this quiet place of solitary prayer our *sanctuary*. Without our sanctuary, it is difficult for us to maintain our sanity while we seek to meet the real needs of our friends and family and live in the rough and tumble events of life. A sanctuary is a safe place; it is a place of refuge from the encroachment of the world. A sanctuary is a place to receive healing from the brutality of the world. Our sanctuary, at its most profound level, is a place of rest and communion where the deepest parts of us connect with the empowering grace and Spirit of God. Like Jesus, our sanctuary is the center we live out of and return to over and over again.

On a personal level, I (Charles) usually seek sanctuary in the silent hours before the rest of the family wakes up. With a cup of freshly-brewed coffee and a Bible in my lap, I quiet my heart and my mind before an ever-present God and welcome

Him into the new day. I rest in His love while I prayerfully read Scripture with the purpose of letting God speak to me from His Word. I finish with the Lord's Prayer and ask for grace that my eyes would see what He wants me to see, my ears would hear what others are truly saying, and my heart and mind would perceive what is real and of true value.

At other times, I find my sanctuary unhurriedly walking in the midst of my neighborhood park, letting God speak to me through His creation. Still other times, sanctuary is found with friends and family laughing and enjoying conversation around the supper table. We will look more closely at this issue of creating space to be loved in chapter five.

While the sanctuary is the place where we meet with God, let Him love us, and receive instruction from Him, quite often it is also in the sanctuary that God lays upon our hearts the desires of His heart—for the world to come to a saving, experiential knowledge of His love for them. Another way of saying this is that we are to live from the sanctuary to the streets. A life in fellowship with the God of the universe will also direct us outward to the mission field of the world.

We may find rest and peace in the sanctuary, but we are called to minister in the streets. For us, the street is wherever we encounter the world. God is as much at home on the streets as He is in the sanctuary. The book of Proverbs speaks of God, personified as wisdom, calling out.

Wisdom calls aloud in the street, she raises her voice in the public squares; at the head of the noisy streets she cries out, in the gateways of the city she makes her speech. (Proverbs 1:20-21)

There is a battle in the streets for the hearts and minds of men and women. Wisdom makes known the ways of God in the streets, but people are often slow to perceive it. Samson did not know when the presence of God had left Him. Moses had to be told he was on holy ground. The people of Jesus' day did not recognize the kingdom of God was in their midst. Jesus, responding to dullness in the people of God, instructed His disciples to travel from town to town and remind the people that the kingdom of God was within their reach—that the kingdom of God was at hand.

The Meat Is in the Street

John Wimber, the founder of the Vineyard movement, used to tell his congregation and anyone else who would listen, "The meat is in the street." In an age of consumerism, Christians can collect spiritual experiences or acquire biblical knowledge and mistakenly believe that spiritual maturity and happiness can be measured by the size of our personal libraries or the strangeness of our religious encounters. The Bible speaks of spiritual growth as moving along a continuum of drinking milk to eating meat. Wimber reminds us that maturity in the Christian life is never relegated to simply acquiring more knowledge or esoteric experiences; it is forever linked to holiness, obedience, and mission—the walking out of our faith. Holiness is obedience turned inward; mission is obedience turned outward. We are called to outwardly focused obedience and, specifically, obedience to the great commission of Christ.

All authority in heaven and on earth has been given to me. Therefore go and make disciples of all nations, baptizing them in the name of the Father and of the Son and of the Holy Spirit, and teaching them to obey everything I have commanded you. And surely I am with you always, to the very end of the age. (Matthew 28:18-20)

Maturity is linked to mission. To move on with God, one must move with God. God moves in the sanctuary to heal the church; God moves in the streets to heal the world. God moves in the sanctuary of our hearts to comfort us; God moves us into the streets to comfort others. The sanctuary is safe, quiet, and peaceful. The street is messy, loud, crowded, dirty and, at times, violent. Wisdom still calls aloud in the streets; she whispers in the schools, she cries out in the suburbs, she raises her voice in the urban areas. The church is to echo the cry of wisdom: "Take off your shoes, you are on holy ground—the kingdom of God is at hand."

We are called to live in the sanctuary and work in the streets. The sanctuary is to be a home we find rest in, but never a gated community from which we seldom venture. We are created to find rest in the sanctuary and to serve in the streets. To hold onto sanctuary and let go of the street is to move toward selfishness. To hold onto the street and let go of the sanctuary is to move toward burnout. To anchor ourselves in both is to encounter God's tender love for us and participate in His compassionate mission in the world.

We have seen many exciting things happen in the sanctuary of the church—lots of healings and demonstrations of God's power; but stirring inside us is a hunger and desire to see the demonstration of God's power expressed beyond the four walls of the church. If it's so good here in the church, it has to be even better out there. It's wonderful whenever God's power is demonstrated in the sanctuary, and we should never discount this because anytime someone is healed or touched by the kingdom of God, it's amazing; but God doesn't want us to keep His presence and power for ourselves. He wants us to freely give what we have received by taking it out to the streets and giving it away. "Freely as you have received, freely give" (Matthew 10:8).

A Friend, a Phone, and a Lady Not Forgotten

I (Brian) recently experienced a powerful encounter in which God radically changed a woman's life "in the streets." Late one night, I was on my way home from a service at church, and I called my friend David Dixon, who lives in Atlanta, Georgia. I kept on hearing *beep, beep, beep.* I asked, "David, are you at a grocery store?" He said yes, he was at Walmart. All of a sudden I received an impression. I didn't have time to think before it came out of my mouth: "Is there a short black lady a little over five feet tall standing in line in front of you?"

He said, "Yeah. What do you have for her?" He sounded a little shocked—but not that surprised. He and I often press in to hear the Lord for others while we're on the phone with each other. We've seen two or three people healed that way. But nonetheless, I was taken aback.

Bewildered, I said, "I don't have anything. I just saw a short black lady in front of you. There really is a lady like that in front of you?" As I said this, I started getting a shooting pain in my lower back going down into my lower hips. I told David I thought there was something wrong with her back going down to her hips.

The thing I love about David is his boldness and his intense desire to press into the kingdom. He was on the other side of the country, and he didn't have any insight from God about this woman. I was in the comfort and anonymity of my van in Oklahoma City while he was smack dab in the line of fire to share the impression I had, risking looking foolish and embarrassed. Because of his passion and desire to see the kingdom of God released, he stepped out boldly.

Over the phone I heard this: "Excuse me, ma'am. I would like to share something with you." A loud commotion started, and I heard a woman emphatically telling David that she didn't want to hear anything he had to tell her. I heard another man join in the ruckus, then the phone call dropped. I thought, *"Oh no! Did I just get my friend in a fight? This must not be God, because there's conflict."* Then I remembered there's always conflict when the kingdom of God is advancing.

After a few moments, I was able to call him back, and I still heard the commotion in the background. "Dude! Are you OK?"

I heard David saying, "Listen, ma'am. I'm a Christian..."

She interrupted him, shouting, "I will have none of that! I was a preacher's daughter, and if you want to go toe-to-toe, we can go toe-to-toe!"

I overheard as he explained, "I don't want to argue with you. I was just minding my own business on the phone with my friend when the Lord described you in detail to him. He said there's something wrong with your back going down into your hips."

I heard the man's voice again as he yelled, "There's nothing wrong with her back!"

But the lady went silent for the first time since the scene began. After a pause, she said, "There is something wrong with my back and hips. Let me talk to your friend."

David handed her the phone, and to be honest, I was freaked out. I was in Oklahoma City and they were in Atlanta at a Walmart check-out stand at 11:00 at night. I started expecting God would give me a download of prophetic information for this woman and it would be amazing, but I didn't receive anything. The lady was on the phone and I explained to her the impression I had about her pain in the lower back and hips. All I felt led to say to her was that God loved her. He had not forsaken her. He was near to her. He knew her situation. He had not forgotten her.

She started yelling and weeping in Walmart: "Oh Jesus! Oh Jesus!"

I just keep telling her how much God loved her.

She finally said, "You don't understand. My husband died a year ago. I have seven children. I thought God left me. I thought He abandoned me. I was a preacher's daughter, so I know better, but why did God take my husband away from me?"

She began pouring out her life to me. The pain in her back was so severe she thought it was literally going to kill her. I just kept telling her how much God loved her.

"I'm just some guy in Oklahoma City, but God loves you so much that He would speak to me while you are in Walmart on the other side of the country to tell you that He is near and that He hasn't forsaken you."

I got off the phone with her, and she continued to talk to David. He prayed for her back, and she experienced healing from the pain. She told David how much this experience had changed her life. She was in such despair over her husband's death that she was ready to commit suicide. She was tired of living until this happened. She continued to call David for a few days telling him how she couldn't believe how God had come near to her.

God intensely desires to meet with us in the sanctuary, but the world will never know how much God loves them until we take what we get in the sanctuary and give it away in the streets.

Insights to Encountering God and Advancing His Purposes

One summer afternoon we found ourselves sitting at a local coffee house talking about the things God had shown us over the years about power ministry. As we began discussing power evangelism, we grabbed a napkin and began writing down those insights that seemed to not only shape our approach to ministry but kept us engaged in evangelism for so many years. These insights have acted as anchors—keeping us from drifting too far from the missional heart of God.

Most of these insights have come to us through the teaching ministry of others; we have simply integrated them into our lives. We have found they have provided us with a framework to better cooperate with God's activity within us and to be more aware of God's activity all around us. Awareness is only part of the challenge; the other is partnering with God as He pours out His love to others. These insights are meant to give structure to our lives to enable us to live an outwardly focused life that is rooted and grounded in the love of Christ. In this chapter we will give a simple overview of the insights. With the rest of the book, we will unpack these insights in more detail.

Insight One: It's All about the Gospel

The gospel message is at the center of everything we do. Mankind was separated from God because of sin. Jesus is the eternal son of God who came to earth as a baby, lived a blameless life, and took the weight and punishment for our sins upon Himself at the cross. Three days later He rose from the dead, overcoming sin, death, and Satan. Through Him we are reconciled to God and can live eternally in fellowship with Him.

Because of the good news, we can rest in the work that Christ has already done for us. We partner with Him not as a means to earn good standing with God, but because He loves us and He loves the people around us. Christ is still at work in the world today and we have the privilege of joining Him in reaching the lost and bringing greater glory to His name.

Our challenge is to keep the message of the Gospel at the center of everything we do, both in our own lives and in ministry.

Insight Two: Learn to Let God Love You

God not only calls us to ministry, He calls us to intimacy as well. Just as a mother and father will spend time together parenting their children, they will also spend time alone together strengthening and deepening their love for each other. It is the same with God. He does not want to simply "use" us for ministry. He loves us, enjoys being with us, and there are times when simply being with Him, apart from ministry activity, is exactly what He wants.

Outwardly focused ministry can only be sustained by an intimate relationship with God. We must develop a prayer life that is intimacy driven, not just ministry driven.

Our challenge is to take time to let God love us and not let the busyness of life or ministry crowd out our relationship with Him.

Insight Three: God Is Always at Work around Us

We don't have to wait for God to do something. He continues to be active in His creation. The Bible tells us that He sustains the created universe by the word of His power. Every breath we take is a gift from God. God's word sustains God's world. God's love is forever reaching out to His world.

We don't bring ministry to others; we participate in the work God is already doing. When Jesus was criticized for healing a lame man on the Sabbath, He explained it this way, "My Father is always at his work to this very day, and I, too, am working" (John 5:17).

Our challenge is to come alongside God and those we are ministering to. We are to learn to listen to God. We must learn to listen deeply to the person and hear what God hears so we can echo God's love back to them.

Our challenge is to live in the reality of God's involvement with the people around us.

Insight Four: The Kingdom of God is at Hand

We don't have to wait for the kingdom of God to come. It has already come in the person and the ministry of Jesus. Jesus' message was fairly simple: The kingdom of God is at hand. The kingdom of God was at the center of Jesus' teaching. Jesus began His public ministry by announcing the kingdom of God was near.

Jesus instructed His disciples to preach the gospel of the kingdom. The twelve apostles (Matthew 10:7) and the seventy-two nameless disciples (Luke 10:1) were all given the same mandate. Following the death and resurection of Christ, Jesus further explained the kingdom to His followers (Acts 1:6-8), Paul taught about the kingdom (Acts 28:31), and the other aspostles and the writer of Hebrews also spoke of the kingdom (2 Peter 1:11, James 2:5, Revelation 1:6, Hebrews 12:28).

Jesus and His disciples did not consign the kingdom of God to the distant future or millennium. He came to usher in the kingdom right now, in our age. We have been called to continue the kingdom mission and ministry of Christ. *Our challenge is to live in the reality of the kingdom of God in our midst.*

Insight Five: We've Already Been Commissioned to Go

We are called to continue the ministry of Jesus. His mission is our ministry. Jesus began His ministry with a simple mission statement:

The Spirit of the Lord is on me, because he has anointed me to preach good news to the poor. He has sent me to proclaim freedom for the prisoners and recovery of sight for the blind, to release the oppressed, to proclaim the year of the Lord's favor. (Luke 4:18-19)

Many of us are waiting for some kind of special word from God or supernatural experience before we find the courage or inclination to step into ministry. Yes, it is important to wait on God, but as a believer, you have already been commissioned. Being a disciple of Jesus means you are His apprentice. An apprentice is called to learn the craft of his master and then continue that craft. Jesus was a healer, a prophet, and an evangelist among other things. He taught the disciples how to do the things He was doing. Before their encounter with Jesus, most of the early disciples were fishermen. As a result of working closely with Jesus, they soon learned how to minister in the power of the Holy Spirit. Supernatural ministry is something that can be learned.

As one reads church history, it becomes clear that the supernatural ministry of Christ has continued from generation to generation. Even during those periods in the church's history when the manifest presence of God's power seemed to diminish, it never disappeared altogether. There have always been those who have stepped into the yoke of empowered discipleship with Jesus and endeavored to continue His mission and ministry in the world.

Our challenge is to stay focused on the mission of Christ in the world and our call to participate in that mission.

Insight Six: Develop the Art of Seeing, Hearing, and Doing

The empowerment to do supernatural ministry is not something we carry around as a personal possession. We cannot drum up a prophetic word or a healing gift at will, nor can we demand it from God. Ministry is not magic. The empowerment to do ministry is the fruit of intimacy with Christ, but intimacy is not enough. We are also required to exercise faith as we step out to do the ministry of Jesus.

Empowered ministry is a working of the Holy Spirit, and experience has taught us that the Spirit gives us grace to minister with His power and gifts as we step out to do ministry and not before. The ability to discern God's activity is like learning a second language: we can hear the words but we don't yet understand the message. Discerning the activity of God is a learned skill and the activation of His supernatural power is usually at the moment of need.

Our challenge is to expectantly watch for God's activity, listen to His voice and discern His will in the present moment.

Insight Seven: Faith is Spelled R-I-S-K

God may empower us on the spot, but He still calls for us to move out in faith. John Wimber was always quick to remind us that faith is spelled R-I-S-K. Even though we believe we may have heard from God, ministry always involves some kind of risk because we are capable of misunderstanding or mishandling what God is trying to communicate to us.

To respond with faith, we usually have to step outside our comfort zone or, at the very least, adjust our immediate plans to respond to God's leading. This always involves taking a risk. There will be times when we get our signals crossed and mishear God.

Our commission is to take a risk and step into the activity of a disciple. We do what we can do in our own strength (listen and pray) and ask God to do what He can do (release His power).

Our challenge is to take risks for the sake of the kingdom.

Insight Eight: The Importance of Routinization

Routinization is the establishment of a pattern or routine. We all love the idea of spontaneity, especially when it comes to showing affection or participating in ministry. However, if left to spontaneity, many important things (such as spending quality time with those we love or attending to unpleasant responsibilities) will go left undone. We all need routine. Even Jesus had set routines in His life (Luke 4:16).

Many of us have established routines that include going to work, raising a family, eating dinner, and worshiping with a faith community. It is also important to establish a routine concerning personal evangelism that emphasizes depending on the Holy Spirit for His power and gifts.

Our challenge is to establish a sustainable Christ-centered routine which includes evangelism.

Insight Nine: Press Through the Pushback

Ephesians 6:12 states:

For our struggle is not against flesh and blood, but against the rulers, against the authorities, against the powers of this dark world and against the spiritual forces in the heavenly realms.

We are in a battle. There are malevolent spiritual beings that wish to keep the world in darkness and do us harm. Evangelism puts us on the front line. The problem with much of Western Christianity is that many of us do not seem to know there is a war going on. When seeking to advance the kingdom of God, conflict is to be expected.

We must learn to fix our eyes on Jesus and allow our focus to remain on Him. The battle will always rage around us; our aim should be to remain Christ-focused in the midst of the storm. He is sufficient in all things, and our focus should never be on the pushback but on the love and mercies of Christ.

Our challenge is to understand the nature of the conflict and then fight with the weapons God has given us, always keeping our focus on Him.

Insight Ten: The "How" Is Just as Important as the "What"

It is important how we do ministry. The way we approach ministry is built on a number of values. Ministry values are like the foundation of a building: they may not be readily seen, but they are present in all we do. Without a clear set of values shaping our ministry, it is too easy, in our enthusiasm, to move toward manipulative practices or attitudes which injure everyone involved. A clear set of biblically based ministry values protects us from doing harm to ourselves and to those we are called to minister to.

Our challenge is to think and pray through a set of biblical ministry values and seek to integrate them into our life and practice.

These insights offer a pattern of life which enables us to walk the balance of being nurtured by the love of God while partnering with Him to accomplish His will through faith and obedience. We hope that they will prove helpful as you take practical steps to partner with God in the ministry of the kingdom. In time, these insights can shape not only how you think, but how you live.

Insight One: It's All about the Gospel

Our challenge is to keep the message of the Gospel at the center of everything we do, both in our own lives and in ministry.

The Gospel Is Good News

As we embark on a journey of a life on mission with God, it is critical that we don't lose the focus of the gospel message. Jesus is the very cornerstone of all we do. The word gospel means "good news." We carry this good news in our hearts, on our tongues, and in our actions: Jesus came to earth as God-in-man, died a gruesome death on a cross in our place so that we could be reconciled to the Father, rose again conquering sin and death, and He now reigns in power with the Father in heaven. This is good news indeed!

Because of our sin, both as a race and each of us individually by choice, we have been separated from God and deserve eternal judgment. His holiness and purity are so great that anything sinful cannot remain in His presence. Yet in His eternal, unrelenting love for us, God desires to save us from our sinful fates and bring us back into relationship with Him. In His divine wisdom and great mercy, God the Father sent Jesus as a means to satisfy both His justice against sin and His love for each of us. In Christ, our sins were lain upon a sinless God who bore our penalty for us, meeting both the demands of God's justice and His love, simultaneously, in one divine act of immeasurable, sacrificial grace. This work that Christ did is called atonement.

Both the love and justice of God come together in the atonement. Without the love God has for us, Jesus would have never taken the steps to redeem us. When Jesus died to pay the penalty for our sins, it showed that God was truly just because He gave the appropriate punishment to sin. Jesus' work of atonement paid the penalty for our sins (1 John 4:10), bore the wrath of God against the horror of sin (Hebrews 9:12-14), reconciled us back into communion with God (2 Corinthians 5:18-19), and broke our bondage to sin and the kingdom of Satan (Colossians 1:13-14).

So if God has done all this in Christ, what are we to do to be saved? Our response can be summarized in two words: repentance and faith (or trust). Repentance means turning away from sin and forsaking sin as best we understand it; faith means turning toward Christ as our living Lord and putting our trust and confidence in Him. Jesus was often moved by the faith He saw in people. The woman with the issue of blood was healed because of her extreme faith in Jesus' ability to heal her (Matthew 9:22). Conversely, Jesus often scolded the disciples for their lack of faith (Matthew 16:8, Matthew 17:20). Jesus expected His followers to trust in the love and power of God.

The amazing paradox is this: even our repentance and faith which lead to salvation are the result of God's goodness toward us. It is the kindness of God which leads us to repentance (Romans 2:4), and He is the one who gives faith (Ephesians 2:8, Hebrews 12:2).

The Good News Turned Inward

As redeemed ones, we must learn to rely on the goodness of God toward us. It was His act of love and mercy which brought us to salvation, and it is His goodness which sustains us as well. We did not do anything to earn salvation and right standing with God, and we cannot, now, do anything to maintain it.

Through the atonement, we are "at one" with Christ. This justifies us (making it just as if we never sinned), and we are declared by God to be not guilty. No amount of striving, no amount of doing, no amount of self-regulation can make me more righteous than I already am. My perfect church attendance record, my list of memorized Bible verses, my timecard of hours in prayer, and the number of people attending my Bible study cannot make me more righteous. In Christ and through Him alone, we have become the righteousness of God (2 Corinthians 5:21). Because of the over-abounding, all-sufficient goodness of God, we are stripped of any ability to do anything to earn, deserve, or add to the righteousness given us through Christ. We are left only to rest in it. To rest in His goodness. To rely on His grace.

Ministry comes out of a place of resting in the goodness and sufficiency of Christ. We may minister out of a conviction of calling, out of gratitude, or out of compassion for others, but never again should we minister out of a desire to prove anything to God or other human beings. All that could be proven was proven on the cross. Our goal is to learn to rest in what He has already done. We do not live a life on mission doing ministry as a means to earn God's favor. We do not pray for the sick or evangelize the lost to prove our righteousness. Rather, because of the cross, we are transformed by goodness into a people so full of gratitude that our lives become clay at the potter's wheel to be used by God as He pleases. We become messengers of the good news because we have partaken of the good news.

The Good News Turned Outward

Jesus came to earth to save us from ourselves and from the oppressions that bind us. Jesus came to give sight to the blind, freedom to the prisoners, and hope to the hopeless. It was good news for the woman at the well (John 4:1-26). It was good news for blind Bartimaeus (Mark 10:46-52). It was good news to Jairus' daughter who was raised from death (Luke 8:49-56). It was good news to the ten lepers (Luke 17:11-19). It was good news to the thief on the cross (Luke 23:39-43). It was even good news to the Pharisees, although they rejected it. It is still good news today.

Our God is a God of compassion. Not only was it compassion for us that compelled Jesus to go to the cross, it was compassion that compelled Him to heal our brokenness. During His earthly ministry, Jesus often acted out of a motivation of compassion. He had compassion on the crowds of people because they were harassed by the enemy and helpless, so He taught them truth (Mark 6:34, Matthew 9:36). He had compassion on the sick, so He healed them (Matthew 14:14). He had compassion for the blind, so He gave them sight (Matthew 20:34). He had compassion on a hungry crowd of people, so He fed them (Mark 8:2). In the story of the prodigal son, the father was filled with compassion for the son, even though it was the son's own choices which had led him to his desperate, destitute state (Luke 15:20).

As we are touched by the good news of the gospel, we too are to be motivated by compassion. We can no longer pass by a hurting person and remain unmoved. We can no longer leave the ignorant to suffer from the pain of their lack of understanding. We can no longer stand by as the lost remain oppressed by the entrapment of sin. It is the compassion and justice of Christ which wells up within us and demands something be done. The good news transforms us into people who are bearers of the reality of that good news.

The life we live is no longer our own; we were bought at a price (1 Corinthians 6:19-20). We are now in Christ and He lives in us. Galatians 2:20 states:

> I have been crucified with Christ and I no longer live, but Christ lives in me. The life I live in the body, I live by faith in the Son of God, who loved me and gave himself for me.

Because Christ lives in us, He carries on His work on the earth through us. His compassion for the hurting has never ceased, and because He lives in us, we are the healing agents through which He seeks to free the oppressed. We are the agents of Christ's good news. We are His ambassadors here on earth, demonstrating the love of Christ for broken humanity despite our own weakness and desperate need for Him.

We evangelize the lost because we have embraced the good news and been overcome by it. We minister out of a place of the overflow of the goodness of God toward us. We are so impressed with what Christ has done for us that we are convinced that only in Christ can the needs of the people around us be met. Only in Christ can the lost be saved, the blind see, the oppressed delivered, the imprisoned freed. It is the conviction of the truth of this good news that compels us into a lifestyle of evangelism. When we understand the good news, we are compelled to share that goodness.

Through Christ's work on our behalf, we are now friends of God, lovers of God. We enter into the benefits of that salvation through simple, childlike trust. Our news is good news: God is a good God and He has taken our sins upon Himself. He has made a way for us to live an abundant life with Him. We need only to receive the good news, trust in Christ, and follow

Him. Our role in ministering to others is to be messengers of this good news in word and deed, in proclamation and demonstration.

One afternoon, I (Brian) went with some friends to a hospital to see if we could serve some people by praying for them. We sought to demonstrate the reality of the good news by bringing healing to people. I saw a man who was standing by the entrance of the emergency room on crutches. He looked really rough, and I could see that his knee was damaged as it was shifted to the right side. I could see the agony and pain, the oppression on him.

I walked over and introduced myself, "My name is Brian, and my friends and I are here doing practical works of service by praying for people. Believe it or not we have seen several people healed today. Jesus wants to release His presence and His love. Do you mind giving me the opportunity to pray for you?" Surprisingly enough, the guy had a really tender heart and let us pray for him.

"I'm going to pray for you and ask the Holy Spirit to come upon you, then I'm going to ask you what you are experiencing, and then I'm going to ask you to do something you couldn't do before. Is that OK?" He agreed, and I prayed briefly for him. Then I asked him what he was feeling.

"I feel this warmth and electricity pulsing through my body," he said with surprise.

"That sounds pretty cool! You weren't experiencing that before I prayed for you, were you?" He said no. "Do you want to try to do something you couldn't do before?"

The guy then handed me both of his crutches and started jumping up and down on the knee that had been twisted and now looked normal. He was crying. "The pain is gone. The pain is gone." He started moving his leg and knee. He was amazed and so was I! We were amazed by the goodness of God. I asked the man, "Do you happen to know Jesus?"

"I know about Jesus, but to be honest with you, I have lived my whole life serving the devil."

I replied, "The devil didn't take the pain out of your knee, Jesus did. There's a lot of pain in your heart, too, and Jesus wants to take the pain out of your heart the same way as He did your knee. Would you like to give your life to Jesus?" He said yes, so I prayed with him to receive Christ into His life. Afterward, he simply turned around and walked off—smile on his face, crutches in his hand, and Jesus in his heart.

It wasn't anything I personally had to offer that changed that man's life. It was the goodness of a God who loved him enough to come and touch his life. Our focus must always remain on the gospel message—both the understanding of our own need for it and the realization that it is the only solution for the hurting, hungry people around us. Our motivation for evangelism is never to feed our own self-righteousness; the motivation is to love God and love people. As we embark on this journey of power evangelism, may we seek to keep the gospel message at the center of everything we do.

Insight Two: Learn to Let God Love You

Our challenge is to take time to let God love us and not let the busyness of life or ministry crowd out our relationship with Him.

In 1994, I (Charles) made a pilgrimage with some friends to Toronto, Canada, to investigate rumors of a revival breaking out in a small Vineyard church. We were not disappointed. Each of us encountered God in powerful ways. The last evening we were there, I heard God's still, small voice whisper to me, *"If you don't let me love you, you won't finish the race."* This word was both a warning and an invitation. When I asked God what "letting Him love me" looked like, I had a mental picture of me holding one of my children in my arms. I felt like God wanted to do the same with me. Just as my children let me love them, He was asking me to approach Him with childlike faith and let Him do the same.

For a few years following that encounter with God, I was careful to set aside time to engage God and intentionally ask that He come and love me. These prayer times were marked by rest and refreshment and at times, new insights into His love for me. But after awhile, the busyness of life and ministry began to push aside these times of intimacy. I continued to pray, but my prayer time became ministry driven rather than intimacy driven. It would take a number of years before the consequence of my lack of intimacy would be fully realized. By 2004, I found myself in a state of serious spiritual decline and emotional burnout.

God is pursuing a love relationship with us, but it is our responsibility to respond. There is a place and need for ministry-driven prayer. Ministry is all about bringing the light of the gospel into the darkness of the world "out there." But God intends to also bring the light of the gospel into the darkness of our own lives, the darkness "in here." In 2004, as I began the long and painful journey out of my spiritual decline and emotional burnout, I returned back to the invitation He gave me in 1994. I began to again set aside time and space for Him to love me. He began to speak to me about prayer not as an activity to perform, but as a place to go to receive. I have written about this in detail in my first two books (*Prayer as a Place* and *Recycled Spirituality*), but let me take a few moments to discuss how to develop an intimacy-driven prayer life and some of the benefits of doing so.

To begin with, this kind of intimate prayer has traditionally been called contemplative prayer. This kind of prayer was common in the early church. In the sixth century, Saint Gregory defined contemplation as simply resting in the love of God. As we learn to live our lives from the sanctuary, contemplative prayer is a means by which we become established in the love of the Father for us.

Contemplative Prayer Is a Place of Intimacy

When I began my own journey into contemplative prayer, one of the first things God told me was to put boundaries around my prayer life. He said, "When we get together, why do we always have to talk about ministry?" He then instructed me not to bring my concerns about the church, the world, my marriage or even my family into this prayer closet. He wanted this time to be about us—Him and me.

This invitation startled me. For so long, my relationship with God was about "doing ministry." My Bible reading was about getting messages for others. Even with my personal relationships with others, I was always good at diverting conversation away from me—what I thought or wanted—and focusing it on others and their needs. All this was a smoke screen to provide cover for my own brokenness. God was interested in me as His beloved. I found that contemplative prayer created a place of intimacy between God and me.

Contemplative Prayer is a Place Where God Drives the Conversation

One of the spiritual disciplines that believers must cultivate is that of listening. One of the greatest gifts we can give anyone is the gift of listening. We have all had the experience of sitting down with someone who does all the talking while we simply nod and smile politely. We intuitively know that they are not interested in anything we have to say; they are only looking for an audience. Recently, in prayer, God spoke to me about the gift of listening. He said that this is a gift that I had learned to give to Him. I was humbled and overwhelmed by what seemed to be His appreciation.

Learning to listen and wait for God to speak is a learned skill. It involves learning to be quiet not just on the outside, but on the inside as well. Ecclesiastes 5:1 reads, "Go near to listen rather than to offer the sacrifice of fools." Learning to listen means that we first learn to quiet our own inner dialogue. We all have an inner critic and a commentator biding for our attention; we must learn to listen for the voice of the Father and let Him lead us beside the still waters and green pastures so that our soul may be restored.

As I have learned to wait for God to initiate the conversation, a couple of things have become apparent. First of all, God is much more interesting than I am. He speaks to us in a myriad of ways: through Scripture, His creation, the counsel of others, the audible inner voice, as well as the still small voice. When He initiates the conversation, He speaks His mysteries into our hearts.

Second, God wants to speak to us about areas and issues we would rather avoid. Many of these conversations have been painful, but the result is always the same—my inner life is being formed into the character of Christ.

A few years back, as I was meditating on Matthew 5:4, "Blessed are those who mourn, for they will be comforted," the Lord spoke to me and told me that I did not mourn. He went on to say that I knew how to deny, pretend and stuff, but I did not mourn. He followed up with a question, *"Why don't you mourn?"*

This running dialogue with God led me into a season of extreme emotional pain. I had spent much of my life denying and dismissing my sorrow and emotional pain, so God took me to Psalms to teach me how to be honest with my disappointments and failures. He uncovered in me a real fear: I was afraid that if I acknowledged and owned my emotional pain, I would fall into a black hole that I would never be able to climb out of. Up to that time, I had made living in denial an art form. I had survived by holding the pain at bay, but in the process I'd begun to shut down emotionally.

In the book *The Wonderful Wizard of Oz* by L. Frank Baum,[2] the Tin Man was a woodsman who came under the spell of a witch. He began to dismember his own body, cutting off his own limbs with his ax and replace the missing pieces with tin. In the end, there was nothing human left—he was a tin man, wishing he had a heart. My own life resembled Tin Man's. Because I was unable and unwilling to face my pain, I began to shut down emotionally—until there was little humanity left. I continued to preach, lead, and go through the motions, but I was dying on the inside.

God took me to the abyss of my sorrow and went into the darkness with me. I began to express my pain and anger with the honesty and irreligiosity of King David. As I did, I began to feel the depth of the pain that I would usually deny. I soon discovered that Jesus did not say, "Blessed are those who mourn, for I will take away their pain." He promised to comfort us in the midst of our pain. My religious tin heart is being replaced with a heart of flesh.

Contemplative Prayer Is a Place Where You Can Process Your Life with God

In the first chapter of Genesis, at the end of each day of creation, God declared it was a good day. He did not have to, but it seemed important to Him to take the time to process each day. The activity of creation was followed by an awareness and appreciation of the significance of what just took place. How many of our days seem to run into each other, when our lives seem to be nothing but a blur?

We all have a myriad of experiences, expectations, confrontations and requests coming our way each day. Some of these feed our souls and make us stronger; other things weaken us and tear us apart. It is important that we learn how to process both the good and the bad in the presence of God and wait for His grace and insight. There is a way to be with God where He helps us debrief; and in that debriefing, He comforts and empowers us to move forward.

Contemplative Prayer Is a Place of Transformation

There is power in the gospel to change us from the inside out. Contemplative prayer is not for cowards. Hebrews 4:12 declares:

> For the word of God is living and active. Sharper than any double-edged sword, it penetrates even to dividing soul and spirit, joints and marrow; it judges the thoughts and attitudes of the heart.

Through contemplative prayer, we discover that the Word of God is living and active. The Word of God becomes a living and energizing force in our lives as believers. The Spirit-filled Word has a life and purpose all its own. It begins to penetrate the defenses and excuses we have set up to resist change. Attitudes and thought patterns that have kept us in bondage and sin become exposed, and through cooperation and God's power, we begin to dismantle everything not rooted and grounded in the love of Christ. James Finley writes:

> We pray not to recharge our batteries for the business of getting back to the concerns of daily life, but rather to be transformed by God so that the myths and fictions of our life might fall like broken shackles from our wrists... Prayer is a death to every identity that does not come from God.[3]

Contemplative Prayer Is a Place of Rest

The early church fathers defined contemplative prayer as simply resting in the love of God. They used the picture of a weaned child simply resting in the arms of his mother. For so many years, my times of prayer were marked by excessive repentance and broken promises to do better in the future. I still repent when God shows me my sin, but rather than promising to do better in the future, I ask God to make me into the kind of person who no longer does the kind of things that do harm to myself and others and bring reproach to His name. I let go of striving and simply rest in His love.

Contemplative prayer lets go of striving and pretending. We learn to be who we are, not who we wish we were or who we think we should be. We learn to be who we are in the presence of God—our sin, our duplicity, our brokenness is no surprise to Him.

There was a time when I operated in a kind of *quid pro quo* mentality. M. Robert Mulholland Jr. speaks of the danger of approaching God the same way we approach a vending machine. But rather than inserting the proper coin, we insert:

> the right technique, the proper method, the perfect program... or we try to create the atmosphere for the right spiritual moment, that perfect setting in which God can touch us.[4]

We do this with the anticipation that we will get what we want from God.

I was taught to put time and emotional energy into prayer, with the expectation that I would be rewarded. I put money into the vending machine of prayer, and I expected an answer when I pulled the lever. It is not too much different from me being nice to my wife during the day with the expectation of intimacy later that evening. Healthy relationships do not work that way. Contemplative prayer is simply learning to rest in the love of God with no strings attached.

Contemplative Prayer Is a Place of Wonder and Surprise

Ephesians 3 speaks of the width, length, height and depth of the love of God. The apostle Paul goes on to declare that God is able to do more than we could ever hope or desire. Contemplative prayer is a way to explore the love that God has for you. Let God surprise you.

We believe that ministry needs to be rooted in intimacy. Call it what you like: resting prayer, soaking prayer, devotional prayer, contemplative prayer, quiet time; the name is not nearly as important as the practice. We all need to set aside a time and place to be regularly encountered and embraced by God.

Jesus, as He was transitioning from a career of faithfully working with His hands as a carpenter to that of an itinerate rabbi, was standing in the water of the Jordan River, being baptized by His cousin John. The Scriptures declare,

As he was praying, heaven was opened and the Holy Spirit descended on him in bodily form like a dove. And a voice came from heaven: "You are my Son, whom I love; with you I am well pleased." (Luke 3:21-22)

This moment of prayer finds Jesus being both empowered by the Holy Spirit and encouraged by His heavenly Father. Jesus and John were both given insight into the nature of God—that He loved His son and was pleased with Him. Following this account, there continues to be a rhythm of Jesus moving into ministry, and then retreating to a quiet and at times an isolated place for the purpose of prayer. The pattern seems to be intimacy, ministry, intimacy, ministry, etc. We would be wise to follow the same pattern. When we become too busy to pray, we have become too busy.

Toward the end of Jesus' public ministry, Jesus was preparing Himself to perform the ultimate service to mankind, offering up His own life as a ransom for ours. Jesus was in a garden speaking to God about His reluctance to follow through with His mission. In Luke's account "an angel from heaven appeared to him and strengthened him" (Luke 22:43). It was in this intimate place of prayer that Jesus was brought back to His mission and found strength beyond Himself to follow through.

God is pursuing a love relationship with us. He has a mission to accomplish through us and a mission to accomplish in us. Both aspects of the mission find fulfillment as we learn to rest in His love. In order to live a life on mission well, we must learn to be rooted and grounded in God's love for us.

Taking Time to Reflect and Respond

At a very deep level, we each need to hear God speak His love and pleasure over us, just as the Father did for Jesus at His baptism. If we slow down to listen, we will find that God delights to pour out His affection on His sons and daughters. In the midst of doing life, we must guard ourselves from being so busy that we don't slow down enough to hear God's words of affirmation and fondness.

When we partner with God in His mission in the world, in the process, we have the opportunity to also grow in our knowledge and intimacy with God. When you partner with God in some kind of activity, He reveals a part of Himself to you. It is important we take the time to process our experiences, to think about what has happened. Speak to God about it, meditate on it, and let God speak to you.

A few years back I (Charles) was at Starbucks getting a latte for the road. The attendant handed me my cup of coffee and then asked me if I wanted a second latte for free. Not one to let a free cup of coffee go to waste, I said yes. My first thought was how much I was going to enjoy both cups of coffee. When I got still on the inside the Lord spoke to me and said, "That coffee is my special gift to Melissa." Melissa was my secretary at the time. I called her on my cell phone to see if she was still at the office and asked her to stay until I returned. I explained the situation to her: that this coffee was God's gift to her, and she was elated. As I pondered this event on my way home, I was overwhelmed with God's love for her as His daughter. Through this simple act of obedience God let me see how affectionate He is toward one of His kids and led me to a deeper intimacy and understanding of the love He has for His children.

One of the best prayer models for reflecting and then processing one's daily life is found in the writings of the Spanish monk, Ignatius of Loyola. Ignatius was born in 1491 to a Basque noble family. After being seriously wounded at the Battle of Pamplona in 1521, while in recovery, he underwent a spiritual conversion. He abandoned his life as a knight and devoted himself to serving God. Spending seven hours a day in prayer, he began formulating a set of Christian meditations and prayers called Spiritual Exercises. For the last 500 years, Christians have been practicing and adapting these spiritual exercises to discern God's activity in their lives.

"The Examen" is an adaptation of one of these exercises. It is a kind of daily debriefing and processing in the presence of God. The Examen is built on the premise that God is involved in our daily lives, forming us into the image of Christ (Romans 8:28-29), and that as we examine our emotional reactions to the day's events, we can discern God voice to us. He identified these emotional reactions as consolations and desolations.

The characteristics of consolations include experiences that encourage, strengthen, and delight us. They are life-giving and life-affirming. They connect us to God, others, and even to ourselves. A practical example would be finishing a conversation with someone and walking away feeling encouraged and affirmed. We are left with a feeling of gratitude and vitality. Desolations would include experiences that drain us, leave us feeling sad, discouraged, overwhelmed or full of anxiety. A practical example would be finishing a conversation with someone feeling emotionally exhausted. The Examen teaches us that God has something to say to us through both our consolations and desolations, and He wants to use both our consolations and desolations as a catalyst to form us into the image of Christ.

I (Charles) practice the Examen by first of all finding a place where I can relax and be quiet. The Examen is best practiced at the end of the day or the beginning of a new day. I acknowledge God's love for me and His involvement in my day (or previous day if practicing the Examen in the morning).

I then ask God to bring to my awareness the moment or event during the day when I experienced the most life and encouragement. I ask God to reveal to me my consolation. If more than one thing comes to mind, I usually ask God which one was the most life affirming or simply choose one myself. I take a few moments to enter back into the joy of that occasion and express my gratitude for what I experienced. Even God took time to enjoy what He had done following each day of creation when He said, "It is good." After a few moments of reflecting and being thankful for the grace of God experienced through the consolation, I ask God what it was about this event that was so life-giving and encouraging. "What would you like to say to me about my consolation?" I sit still and wait for His response. Many times I will journal this part of the exercise.

I then ask God to bring to my awareness the moment or event during the day that drained life out of me, that left me discouraged or full of anxiety. I ask God to reveal to me my desolation. If more than one thing comes to mind, I ask God to show me which one He would want to speak into. I take a few moments to enter back into the pain of that event and relive my feelings without trying to change or mentally fix it in anyway. Rather than deny or stuff my pain, I honestly acknowledge it before God. Jesus tells us, "Blessed are those that mourn, for they will be comforted." I then ask God to show me what it was about the event that caused me to feel so hopeless, discouraged or sad. I ask Him to speak into it and give me His perspective, and then I wait. Many times, I will journal this part of the exercise. I then ask God to come and comfort me and fill me with His love. I sit in silence for a few moments and soak in His presence.

I finish this exercise giving thanks to God for both being with me in my consolations and desolations. I have been practicing this exercise for more than five years. It has taught me how to slow down and process my experiences before God rather than simply letting life become a blur of activity. The Examen helps create a sense that each of our days is sacred because God is intimately involved in our lives. I think David Benner says it best when he writes,

> *We cannot attain the presence of God. We're already totally in the presence of God. What is absent is awareness. This is the core of the spriritual journey— learnining to discern the presence of God, to see what really is... Most of us learn to discern God's pressence by first looking for it in the rearview mirror. That is the value of a prayerful review of the day.*[5]

Signs, Wonders, and Mosquitoes

During our first trip to Romania in 2004, I (Brian) became aware of an amazing way in which Jesus was pouring out His love on a young man. You have all heard the legends about vampires in Romania. Guess what? The legends are true—there really are vampires in Romania. Those blood-sucking vampires are called mosquitoes! Romanian mosquitoes are vicious.

One of the young German teenage boys was severely bitten all over, so much so that the bites had become infected. He was in pain and discomfort. During one of the ministry times, we prayed for this young man. The power of God came over him, so much so that he fell on the ground and stayed there for quite a while. I didn't think much of it at that time, but the next morning his dad came to me and told me the rest of the story.

"After you prayed for him, he had a vision where he had an encounter with Jesus. Jesus invited him to swim in a golden lake. After he swam, Jesus invited him into a room where there was a table of food. He saw a chalice with wine and bread—the elements of communion. Jesus said, 'Drink this, eat this. It will heal your mosquito bites.' So Jesus served him communion. After he came out of the encounter, he was completely healed of his mosquito bites."

Jesus not only desired to heal this boy's body of the infection from the mosquito bites, but He did it in a personal way in which the boy encountered Jesus and His love. God not only desires to do things for us but to also work in us and with us.

Obedience Rooted in Love

Central to Jesus' relationship with God the Father was obedience rooted in love. Jesus, speaking of His relationship with God the Father said, "I love the Father and do exactly what my

Father has commanded me" (John 14:31). Jesus obeyed the general instruction and counsel of Scripture, but beyond that, He also obeyed the daily commands of His Heavenly Father. Out of that relationship marked by love and obedience, greater intimacy and insight flowed. "For the Father loves the Son and shows him all he does" (John 5:20).

Obedience rooted in love is to mark our relationship with God as well. For the Christian, obedience is embedded in love. Obedience to the mission of Christ without love is cold and lifeless. It is like a faux fireplace. Although it may look like something is burning, there is no warmth. A lifestyle of serving God without being rooted in His love breeds either pride and a religious facade or anxiety and burnout.

Anything short of obedience rooted in love is at best an anemic form of Christianity. Jesus tells us,

> If you love me, you will obey what I command...If anyone loves me, he will obey my teaching. My father will love him, and we will come to him and make our home with him. (John 14:15,23)

Jesus promises a kind of familial intimacy with God to those disciples whose obedience is the fruit of their love. None of us, apart from Jesus, are able to fully maintain the kind of intimacy God wants from us; but we can learn to live in the balance of letting God love us while we also partner with Him in His mission to the lost world.

Insight Three: God Is Always at Work around Us

Our challenge is to live in the reality of God's involvement with the people around us.

Drive-thru Healing

Late one night, I (Brian) was going through a Taco Bueno drive-thru, indulging my late-night cravings. As I was at the window and the lady was giving me my food, I had three very faint, fleeting impressions pop in my mind: I felt that there was something wrong with her neck, her stomach, and she was having migraine headaches. There was nothing in the natural that indicated that she had any health problems. Simultaneously with the impressions, my mind began to race with other thoughts as well. *How do I share these impressions? I have maybe fifteen to thirty seconds. I've got people in line behind me, and what if I'm wrong? Am I going to look foolish? I'm going to look like this insane guy that says God speaks to him. But what if these impressions are God at work? If I do share this, maybe God has something for this lady.*

I grabbed her attention by asking her for more napkins. (To be honest, I was stalling a bit.) When she came to the window, I said, "I know this sounds crazy, but sometimes I get pictures and impressions for people." She had the classical deer-in-the-headlights look, which I have grown accustomed to by now. "I sensed that there is something wrong with your neck and your stomach, and you have migraine headaches." As I shared that, another piece of information came: "This has been primarily happening in the last week."

Tears filled her eyes as she said yes.

I said, "The only reason I would know this is because Jesus wants to come near to you. May I have your hand?" (I wasn't proposing to her—I just haven't established a good protocol for praying for people in Taco Bueno drive-thru's yet.)

I reached my hand out to her, with people waiting in line behind me and my MexiDips and chips getting cold in the front seat of my car, and I began to pray a very short prayer. "Jesus, would you come near to her? Would you come and touch her? Let your presence come upon her, and let her know you are near to her." As she began to weep I calmly said, "That's all. Jesus just wanted you to know that He's real and He's near, and He knows what's going on in your life." I drove off as she was wiping away her tears.

In the midst of the busyness of our lives, it is easy to forget that God is actively involved in the lives of people around us. I didn't set out that evening to pray for anybody. I just wanted some food. But I have learned to recognize God's activity in the lives of people around me. We often have many interactions with people in a day—our family members, co-workers, friends, the man at the grocery store register, the woman bothering us with a solicitation phone call during dinner. Without exception, God has a plan for each of these people and He is actively, intimately involved in their lives to work toward the end which He desires. He loves them immensely and dreams more for them than they are able to dream for themselves. He desires to bless them, calling them out of darkness and into His light. If our desire is to be Christ's ambassadors on earth—not merely seeking to minister to people out of pious compulsion or in order to put another proverbial notch in our religious belts—then we must learn to look at people through the lens of God's love for them. We can rest in the knowledge that God is always actively and lovingly involved in the lives of the people around us. Our job is to simply join Him in His activity.

God's Divine Plan

Because God is actively involved in reaching every person with His love, He has a divine plan to bring them into fellowship with Himself. Evangelism must operate out of dynamic relationship with the Father. Otherwise we just set out to make converts and bully our way into their lives, often leaving more destruction in our wake than true revelation of the love of the Father. However, a heart for evangelism cultivated from intimacy with the Father puts us in the position of being co-laborers with Christ. He has a plan and we get the privilege to tag along in what God is already doing in that person's life. As co-laborers, we can allow Christ to do the heavy lifting of making a plan to reach the person. We often stumble along that predestined plan as we join with Christ in His work to reach those around us.

Dianna Bello (Charles's wife) shares a great story that illustrates this dynamic.

> The day began as uneventful as most, when I received a call from my friend Patty. She had been invited to speak with one of her daughter's troubled friends, so she asked me to come along for some support. I really didn't want to go. It was an hour away, and I wasn't feeling all that spiritual or loving toward a stranger that day; but because Patty was a friend and I enjoyed hanging out with her, I decided to go.

> We met up with the young mother at a park near her trailer home. She had two small children, and Patty had brought along her granddaughter to play with the woman's kids. The park was a good call. During our play

date, the young mother asked all kinds of questions about life, God, and hearing His voice. She was very interested in trying to be the best mom she could be. Her husband (or maybe it was her boyfriend) was in jail and she was desperate for answers pertaining to life and God. She had some kind of knowledge of God from her grandmother as a small child, but never grew in her faith.

We found ourselves back at the trailer; the kids had had enough fun at the park. She was very grateful for us coming and spending time with her. We asked her if we could pray for her before we left, and she agreed. The kids started going a little crazy during the prayer, they started bickering and fighting and grabbing food out of the unpacked groceries. We proceeded and we blessed her. We asked God to give her everything she needed, and we ask for God to reveal Himself to her in ways she could identify so that she could begin to experience the life He had for her.

It was a nice prayer. She felt blessed and thankful for us to have come out and spent so much time with her and her kids, even as they wreaked havoc during our prayer time. She stated she wasn't absolutely sure she could really hear God's voice if He did speak. Upon hearing this, I just asked to say one more little prayer of blessing on her ears, specifically that God would open her ears to hear Him. She agreed. As we began to bless her ears she gasped and shouted out that she could hear!

What we didn't know is she was deaf in one ear since she was a small child. God opened her deaf ear! She could hear! We didn't even know what we were praying for, and yet God did according to His will and plan. It was awe-inspiring to be a part of such a miracle.

Dragging many of her friends with her, she went to church the following week. After the service, she approached the pastor requesting to be baptized. Her journey had been reignited by the power of God and by the willingness of two strangers to share their lives' journeys with her and pray for her.

Dianna and Patty didn't know the key to this woman's heart would be prayer over her ears. They simply stumbled upon it as they were obedient to partner with Jesus in His plan. Jesus knew about her ears and it didn't matter whether Dianna did or not. He had a plan in place before these women ever met. Likewise, we can rest in the knowledge that God's love extends so overwhelmingly to everyone we encounter that He will give us the keys we need when we need them.

Examining Our Worldview

Though we may believe theologically that God is actively involved in the world around us, why is it so difficult for many of us to live in the reality of that knowledge? Why do we go through our day to day lives unaware, oblivious to His activity in our neighbor, our waitress, or our boss? For many Western Christians, this is tied to our worldview; we are simply conditioned to not see beyond what our five senses tell us.

A worldview is a way of seeing reality. It is the lens through which we look as we gaze at life. This lens filters, colors, and distorts our perception of the world around us. Our worldview includes our beliefs, attitudes, assumptions, values, and ideas about the world, ourselves, and life in general. Our worldview answers the most basic question: "What is real?" Worldview is like hardened cement, it is very difficult to change once it has been set into place during the early years of our lives.

We simply react reflexively to the world around us through this lens.

Many factors influence our worldview. Most obviously is the culture we grew up in—including our national culture, family culture, church culture, ethnic culture, and generational culture. Our experiences (both those we have and those we lack) shape our worldview. Also, because of the fall, sin has distorted our view of reality. This holds true for those of us who are followers of Jesus. Even though we have been redeemed from sin, we still must contend against ungodly ways of thinking.

Most people in North America and Western Europe, both Christian and secular, have inherited a worldview that was largely formed in the seventeenth century. This viewpoint compared the world to a machine. God, if He existed, created the universe like a huge clock. He wound it up in the beginning, set in motion and then walked away and is now letting it run down. If one is a Christian, then room was made for God, from time to time, to reach down and intervene. This intervention was seen as a miracle. God the outsider interacts with His creation on rare occasions, but this is usually the exception, not the rule.

Jesus' view of reality was much different. It encompassed much more than can be observed with the five senses of sight, hearing, touch, taste, and smell. Jesus acknowledged the existence of a spiritual realm, and He interacted with it as easily as He interacted with the natural, material world. This unseen realm, inhabited by angels, demons, and Satan, was just as real to Him as the physical world. Jesus waged war against the powers of darkness, and He did so in both the spiritual and physical realms by healing the sick, casting out demons, forgiving sins, and preaching the kingdom of God.

Our challenge as Western believers seeking to grow into the image of Christ is to learn to see and operate in this unseen realm. Unfortunately, we quite often miss what God is doing around us simply because it is outside our expectations. Our worldview teaches us to expect very little intervention from God in our lives and the lives of those around us, so we are often simply blind to His activity. As Job 33:14 states, "For God does speak—now one way, now another—though man may not perceive it." The problem is not the lack of God's activity in our world; the problem is our inability to perceive it.

The low expectations generated by our worldview place a veil over our eyes blocking our view of the reality of God's active, loving involvement all around us. Our ability to see into the supernatural realm and begin to operate in signs and wonders will not come naturally to us. Like a second language, it must be learned. We must hold our worldview with open hands out to the Lord, allowing Him to shape and mold it into His way of thinking and doing. As Paul admonishes us in Romans 12:2,

> *Do not conform to the pattern of this world, but be transformed by the renewing of your mind. Then you will be able to test and approve what God's will is—his good, pleasing and perfect will.*

Changing Our Worldview

Even though we are formed and shaped by our worldview, we are not trapped within it. Our worldview will always influence us. But we can learn to live and think differently. As we are on this quest to be conformed into the image of Christ and see the world around us as He does, we must make the choice to change the way we think. We must learn to take every thought captive to the obedience of Christ (2

Corinthians 10:5). We must decide that in order to become more like Jesus we must see the world and see people the way He does. Here are a few suggestions about how to go about changing your worldview.

1. Recognize that we are dependent upon the Holy Spirit. We need God's grace to be able to see the kingdom of God and His activity in the lives of those around us. Pray and ask God to give you eyes to see.

2. Spend lots of time in Scripture, especially in the Gospels and Acts. As you read, put yourself into the stories you read. Read with the understanding that what God did then, He still does now. God is unchanging, so build an expectation that the same God who did what you read in Scripture desires to do the same types of things now.

3. Make sure there is no sin or unwillingness on your part causing you to hold onto wrong ways of thinking. Check your motives and attitudes toward the things of God, especially regarding signs, wonders, and miracles. We have all seen abuses of power by people claiming to act on God's behalf, but we cannot allow their sins to justify our unwillingness to let God change us, and love the world through us in the ways that He desires.

4. Count the cost of making this shift. It is counter-cultural—and this often includes our church cultures—to contend for the reality of the kingdom of God in our lives. It requires some sacrifice to believe God for healing and miracles and signs and wonders. To move to a more supernatural perspective is to go against the grain of what most western Christians believe. Part of the price we must pay involves willingness to risk reputation for truth and to accept the fact that embracing Jesus' worldview may have negative

consequences in terms of fitting in with our present faith community.

5. Give yourself opportunities for new experiences. Because our worldview is so closely linked with our experiences, begin to choose to engage in activities that will help you gain new experiences. It is one thing to know that God can do something and quite another to see Him do it through you. Get around people who are operating in power evangelism and join them. It's okay if you start small, just start!

Who's the Real Chicken?

In the mid 1990s, I (Brian) could count on one hand the people who I knew were actually operating in power evangelism in the streets. I had personal experience of God being active in our church services, but I was hungry to see God's power at work outside the safety of a church event. Up to that point, I hadn't really seen God moving "in the streets." Being part of the Vineyard movement, I had heard all these incredible stories about a man named Blaine Cook. Blaine was a hero of mine in the faith. His personal stories of releasing the power of God in personal encounters with people outside the church stirred up the evangelist in me. I had heard that he would be sharing at a Vineyard church in Chicago, so with a couple of friends, Greg Roberson (a Vineyard pastor) and David Mullikin, I drove from Oklahoma City to Chicago, hoping to gain from his insight and gifting.

Personally, I was really hungry to see this activated in my life. For a couple of years, my wife and I had been attending the Oklahoma City Vineyard church and were familiar with the Vineyard five-step healing model taught by John Wimber. We were seeing healings and demonstrations of God's power within the church, but I wanted to see more. I wanted to see the power of God outside the church. I reasoned that perhaps if I could get around someone who was doing it, something would rub off.

So, the three of us took off for a fourteen hour drive to Chicago to see Blaine Cook. I remember the atmosphere in the car being charged with excitement. The three of us had lots of faith and expectation. My heart's cry was, *"Oh God, please use me. I want to be used by you to do power evangelism. Oh God, please impart your power."*

We arrived and settled in, and the next morning we attended the first session. To my surprise, Blaine pointed me out of the crowd of hundreds and declared, "God is going to use this man powerfully in power evangelism."

At that moment the power of God came on me so strongly that I shook and fell to the ground. On the floor, I was overjoyed and thought, *"Wow! God heard my prayer! He even used a hero of mine to call me out and speak an impartation!"* I could not believe it. I was so filled with faith. I continued to cry out for God to use me for evangelism and give me opportunities to step out in faith.

During our lunch break, the opportunity I prayed for came. Greg, David, and I went to Popeye's Chicken for lunch. As we walked into the restaurant, I noticed a woman standing in line, and immediately pain began to shoot down my right arm. I had an impression that God wanted me to pray for this woman and release healing to her arm. One would think that I would have been full of faith and excitement in light of the encounter I had that morning and the cry of my heart to be used by God just hours ago. Remember, I had just been called out publicly by a hero of mine who had been used tremendously in power evangelism. I had driven across the country asking for such an encounter. But in the midst of this opportunity, I began to doubt. I told myself, *"This isn't God. This is just my imagination."*

My friend Greg noticed the troubled and puzzled look on my face, and he asked me what was going on. I explained to Greg what I thought I had been given by God and that I believed if we prayed for the woman, her arm would get healed. Greg told me, "What are you waiting for? Go over and tell her what God said and pray for her."

"NO WAY!" I told him, "I'm not doing that! What if this is just my imagination? What if I am wrong?"

"OK, then," Greg replied, "I'll go ask her if your impression is right."

I replied, "Only on one condition. You cannot tell her that the impression came from me."

One of the things I love about Greg is that he is fearless. Greg was not called out in a public meeting, and he didn't get an impartation from God. He did not even get the impression for the woman in line. Yet he had more faith than I had. Greg marched up to the woman as I tried to hide so the woman would not see me. I know as you are reading this you might be thinking, *"What a chicken!"* I can only agree with you. The chickens being served for lunch that day were not the only chickens in the restaurant.

Greg tapped the woman on the shoulder and she turned around. Greg told her, "See that guy over there," as he pointed directly at me. "He is a friend of mine, and he felt like the Lord told him that you have a pain in your right arm, and God wants to heal you." I was embarrassed and cursing Greg in my mind. The woman told Greg that her right arm was hurting her. Greg asked if he could pray for her. She said yes. So right there in line,

Greg prayed for the woman. The woman excitedly declared "The pain is gone!" God healed her on the spot.

Rather than rejoicing in God's graciousness over this healing as I should have done, I immediately thought, *"You chicken! THAT COULD HAVE BEEN YOUR TESTIMONY!"* That day I learned this valuable lesson: God is always at work around you, even when you are a chicken.

Walmart Double Bonus Day

A few weeks after my trip to Chicago, when I found out that I was an anointed chicken instead of a mighty man of faith, I was shopping at Walmart with my friend, Jon. We were looking for fishing equipment, but God had bigger plans. He was intending to teach me about His fishing equipment and give me another opportunity to learn to become a fisher of men. Jon and I were simply walking through the store; we were talking and just hanging out. We were not talking about spiritual stuff, just talking about life.

One of the Walmart employees walked up to us and asked if we needed any help. We said, "No, we're just hanging out and looking around." The employee continued to follow up and was persistent about wanting to help us find something. (Isn't it funny when you go to a store and need assistance you can never find anyone, but when you want to be left alone they won't leave you alone?) So, being the nice, sweet Christian that I am, I eventually turned to him with a stern look on my face and said, "Leave us alone—we don't need anything." The employee turned around and walked off. My tone and attitude were clearly in a state of annoyance and I was obviously being a jerk.

As he was walking away, I had the impression that this guy had a pain or irritation in his eyes, and I needed to go and pray for him. My first thought was, *No way! How can this be? I was so rude to him!* But then I remembered what happened a few weeks prior at Popeye's Chicken. *What if this really is God and not my imagination? I don't want to chicken out again.* So now I had two hurdles to jump over. First, I had to overcome my fear and doubt, and second, I had to overcome being a jerk to this guy just moments before.

I decided that I would take a risk, so I went looking for the employee. I located him, but to make matters even worse, he was not alone. There were other employees around him. I drummed up my courage and walked up to the group and spoke to the man. I said, "Excuse me. You are never going to believe this, but I am a Christian, and sometimes God speaks to me." I tried to act like a professional evangelist, but this was actually only the second time this had ever happened to me in public, and the first time I had chickened out.

I apologized to him for being rude, and then I told him that when he turned and walked away, I began to have a burning sensation in my eyes. As soon as I said these words, another set of words came out of my mouth before I could catch them, "You have had this condition for two weeks in your eyes and I believe God wants to heal you right now. Can I pray for you?"

He told me that my impression was correct and I could pray for him. I could not believe it! To begin with, I was correct in hearing the word of knowledge, and second, he was going to let me pray for him even though I had been a jerk. I suggested we go to an aisle that wasn't crowded with people so I could pray for him.

I asked him to hold out his hands. After all, this is how we usually prayed for people in church; I was still a novice at praying for people in public. I prayed, "Holy Spirit, come and release your healing on this man now." What happened next no one had ever prepared me for. After my short prayer, the man began to heave very loud breaths in and out. I did not know what to do, so I just stood there watching him. After a few moments of this I asked him, "Hey man, how are your eyes?"

He responded, "I can breathe! I can breathe!"

"I wasn't praying for your breathing, I was praying for your eyes," I said, bewildered.

"You don't understand. I haven't been able to breathe like this for months. I can breathe! I can breathe!" Then I asked him again about his eyes, "They are fine too!"

To be honest, I was completely shocked and puzzled by what had just transpired. I didn't know what to say or what to do next. So I said, "Well, I guess its double bonus day for you, dude!" And I walked away, shaking my head, completely blown away by what just happened.

You may be thinking, *You could have led this guy to Jesus! Not only are you a chicken, and a jerk, you are stupid!* Yes, I would probably agree with you now, but at the time I was so shocked with what happened, I did not know what to do. This was only my second experience with the power of God outside of the church walls.

This encounter proved to be a watershed moment for me. There was a profound shift in the tectonic plates of my worldview. There was no turning back; I now knew by experience that God is willing and able to do in the streets what I had only seen Him do in church.

Insight Four: The Kingdom of God Is at Hand

Our challenge is to live in the reality of the kingdom of God in our midst.

The Mission of God

The God of the Bible is a God on a mission. God is not content to be an absentee landlord; He is intimately involved in the life and the affairs of His people. He is actively reconciling the world to Himself and He uses men and women to partner with Him in that mission.

Reading through the Bible, we discover that through Abraham, God revealed Himself as One who wants to bless all the nations of the world. Through Moses, God revealed Himself as the deliverer who hears the cries of His people. Through David, God revealed that His Seed would rule all nations and His kingdom would be for all peoples. Through Isaiah God revealed that His salvation would reach the ends of the earth and that a new people would be formed out of every nation. Through Daniel, he said the coming kingdom of God would break all the kingdoms of the earth into pieces and a new "messianic age" would be ushered in. Through John, God revealed that people from every nation, tribe, tongue and people would worship Him forever. Scripture is filled with examples of God partnering with human beings to bring forth His will on earth.

Instead of carrying out His mission on His own, God chooses to partner with people to accomplish His purposes. He initiates a relationship with us because He loves us. In that context of His love for us and for others, He invites us to partner with Him in His mission in the world.

A Hotel Room and the Kingdom of God

After checking in at a hotel, I (Charles) hurried to the sauna in order to relax. As I was settling into the wet heat, I was joined by a man in his early thirties. After we exchanged greetings, I quietly prayed, asking God to give me a door into this man's life. The first thing that popped into my mind was to talk about marriage, so I asked him if he was married, and he said that he was. This led into a discussion on the trials that all marriages face. I shared with him how God was transforming me as a husband and how I was learning to love my wife unconditionally. Somewhere in the conversation he shared with me that he had attended church as a small child, but as an adult, he saw no need for church or God. But in spite of his lack of interest in God or the church he remained extremely engaged in our conversation.

The effects of the heat and appointments we both had cut our conversation short, but we agreed to meet together again the following morning for breakfast at the hotel restaurant.

Early the next day, I made my way to the restaurant and found an empty table, wondering if I would be eating alone. The restaurant was noisy with conversation and clattering cups and dishes. To my delight, my new found friend walked into the restaurant and made his way to my table. As he sat down, his countenance told me that he had just experienced a sleepless night and was troubled. We made small talk, and then I asked if he would rather find a quieter place to talk. We went to his room, and he sat on the bed while I pulled up a chair and he began to share his story.

He had been married for less than ten years, and he had felt much of the life of his marriage had evaporated. He had met a single woman a number of months earlier, and they had begun developing a romantic relationship. In fact, the reason he was in town was to take this relationship to the next level (sexual intimacy). Upon leaving the sauna the day before, he went to her apartment with the express purpose of consummating their relationship. He went on to share that our conversation about God and marriage had taken the wind out of his sails, and not to be overly explicit, he shared that his sexual passion and desire for this woman was no longer there. He found that he was impotent to perform. She was both angry and confused. He left her apartment and spent the night alone in his hotel room, waiting for the morning to come so we could talk.

Upon hearing his story, I informed him that God had protected him from a serious mistake. I went on to tell him that our meeting was a divine encounter orchestrated by God, and I shared the gospel with him. To my surprise, he told me that he was not ready to surrender his life to Jesus. I responded by taking the Gideon Bible out of the nightstand next to his bed, reading some key verses, and again explaining the need to come into right relationship with Christ. Again, he told me he was not ready or willing to surrender to God.

At this point, I was extremely frustrated. I was certain that the Holy Spirit had given me an inroad into this man's life and that God was actively drawing him to Himself. With more frustration than faith, I asked this man if I could pray for him, and he gave me permission. I prayed the prayer Jesus taught His disciples to pray: "Let your kingdom come." To my surprise the young man began to shake violently. He literally began bouncing on the bed in a seated position. After watching this spectacle for a few moments, I asked him again, "Are you ready to surrender your life to the lordship of Christ now?"

He replied in a shaky voice, "YEEESSSSS."

I asked him to speak to God himself and to surrender with as much integrity as he could at the moment. As he prayed, the violent shaking stopped and he began to experience the love of God being poured into his heart. We then spent some time talking about what he would do when he returned home and the kind of church he needed to look for in order to grow in his new-found faith.

In sharing this story, I am not implying that saying "Let your kingdom come" is some kind of formula or a kind of Christian incantation that causes a release of spiritual power. I simply prayed the prayer God wanted me to pray at that moment. God had been reaching out to this man his whole life; he was emotionally bankrupt, and his marriage had come to a place of crisis. By God's providence, I was in this man's life as God's ambassador with the good news that the kingdom of God was at hand.

The Kingdom of God Is at Hand

The belief that God is always at work around us is closely tied to the message Jesus most often preached: "The kingdom of God is at hand!" Throughout the Gospels, in the many accounts of Jesus' preaching, this is the one message we see Him repeating over and over—the nearness of the kingdom of God. The message of the kingdom of God was the centerpiece of Jesus' teaching and activity.

We tend to think of kingdoms today in terms of geographical boundaries; but a kingdom can be more accurately described as the area in which a king's rule and reign is being demonstrated. In other words, wherever the will of the king is done, his kingdom has been established in that place. So when speaking of the kingdom of God, we are speaking of the establishment of the rule and reign of God on the earth. Jesus proclaimed this message: the rule and reign of God is here! It isn't consigned to another time or another place. It is literally "at hand"; it can be grasped. It is knocking at the door and is within reach of those who want it.

Because the rule and reign of God is something which cannot always be seen with our physical eyes, Jesus went about describing it in parables. It is like treasure hidden in a field. It is like a tiny mustard seed which grows into a huge tree. It is like yeast which makes its way through the whole loaf of bread (see Matthew 13:1-52, Mark 4:1-34, and Luke 13:18-21). Each of these was a way of describing the all-consuming power and immeasurable value of the reality of the kingdom of God on earth.

Proclamation plus Demonstration

Jesus didn't just talk about the kingdom of God—He demonstrated it! He was an expert at show and tell. He would proclaim the nearness of the kingdom of God, and then He would demonstrate the reality of the truth of which He spoke by doing the works of the kingdom, like healing the sick, cleansing the lepers, and freeing those oppressed by demons. This pattern is repeated over and over in the Gospels. He would tell the people that the kingdom of God was at hand, and then, in practical ways, He would show them exactly what this meant for their lives. The presence of the kingdom meant total freedom to those trapped in the shackles of demonic oppression. It meant the decimation of sickness and disease. It meant sight for the blind and hearing for the deaf. It meant that the lame, when touched by the power of the nearness of the kingdom, could leave leaping and praising God. Jesus did not consign the kingdom of God to the distant future. He understood that the kingdom of God is a present reality, active in our present age.

Matthew 4:23-24 gives a summary of Jesus' ministry:

Jesus went through Galilee, teaching in their synagogues, **preaching the good news of the kingdom**, *and* **healing every disease** *and sickness among the people. News about him spread all over Syria, and the people brought to him all who were ill with various diseases, those suffering severe pain, the demon-possessed, those having seizures, and the paralyzed, and he healed them. Large crowds from Galilee, the Decapolis, Jerusalem, Judea and the region across the Jordan followed him. (Emphasis added. See also Matthew 9:35-36.)*

Throughout the Gospels, there is a clear pattern of ministry that unfolds: proclamation and demonstration. Jesus preached repentance and the good news of the kingdom. He accompanied the proclamation of the kingdom with a demonstration of the power of God. Jesus healed the sick, drove out demons, discerned the secrets of men's hearts and raised the dead. The message of the kingdom was more than words. There was an actual impartation and manifestation of the presence and power of God.

The Kingdom Is Both Now and Not Yet

Jesus proclaimed a kingdom which is both present and future at the same time. God's kingdom was present in His ministry, but it was not fully present. This is an uncomfortable paradox that we as disciples of Jesus must learn to live in and accept. The future kingdom has broken in but has not yet been fully established. The kingdom is really here but not fully here. Satan, sin, death, and suffering are yet to be fully destroyed. Jesus healed the sick and raised the dead, yet He Himself was beaten and nailed to a tree. We are still living in a present evil age where sickness, oppression and sin still exist, but the future age has already begun breaking in through the ministry of Christ and His church.

There will be a day in which the kingdom of God will fully come—the day when every knee shall bow and every tongue confess that Jesus Christ is Lord (Philippians 2:10-11, Isaiah 45:23). On that day, all oppression will cease, death will be no more, and Christ will reign on the earth. So in that respect the kingdom is not yet here. Yet Jesus preached the reality of that very kingdom now.

So we must live in this tension. We cannot deny the truth of Jesus' message that the kingdom of God is at hand. In Christ there is healing, deliverance, salvation, and freedom. Yet at the same time, the full manifestation of these things is still to come. Our challenge is to maintain this tension—to hold on to both the now and the not yet of the kingdom. If we cling to only the now of the kingdom we will become discouraged when we experience anything short of complete healings, deliverances, and salvations. On the other hand, if we trust only in the future aspect of the kingdom of God, we miss the opportunity to partner with Him now to bring the kingdom into our lives and the lives of those around us.

Don Williams, in his book, *Signs, Wonders, and the Kingdom of God* writes:

> *The reason why this truth is so gripping is that it illumines so much of our present experience. It explains both our sense of triumph in Christ and the continuing spiritual*

warfare which we fight on many fronts. It explains the reality that we have died with Christ and, at the same time, that the flesh still wars against the spirit. It explains why people are dramatically healed today by the power of God and also continue to get sick and die. It explains why we have strength through weakness and life through death. If we break the tension we either end up in perfectionism, on one hand, or despair, on the other. The good news is that the future kingdom is now at work in the present and that we are enabled to live between the times.[6]

The kingdom of God is active in this present evil age, bringing the blessings of the age to come. The future is breaking into the present everytime a person is healed. The kingdom of God is at hand every time a demon is driven out. The kingdom of God has come every time a broken relationship is reconciled. Every time someone leaves their self-centered life and surrenders to the lordship of Christ, they have left the domain of darkness and entered into the kingdom of God. When the kingdom invades our present life, we get a foretaste of the power of the age to come. There will come a day when the kingdom comes fully in power and authority, but we live in the "now but not yet." The kingdom has already come, but not yet in its fullness.

The church's role in all of this is to continue to proclaim the message and ministry of the kingdom. The church is called to expand the kingdom of God into the nations of the world. When this is accomplished, we can expect the kingdom of God to come in its fullness.

And this gospel of the kingdom will be preached in the whole world as a testimony to all nations, and then the end will come. (Matthew 24:14)

As citizens and ambassadors of His kingdom, every time we heal the sick, comfort the dying, step out in faith, evangelize the lost, teach the inquisitive, give ourselves to the poor, stand up for the oppressed, and care for the orphan and widow, we are declaring through our words and actions that the kingdom of God is at hand.

The Kingdom of God at a Bar

Late one night, I (Brian) was on the phone with my friend Greg Roberson, who was a security guard. He was on duty at a shopping center which had a bar. While we were talking, I heard a man come up to Greg and say something to him. As he spoke, I sensed an impression that the man had an upper respiratory problem. I shared this with Greg.

Greg said the guy looked normal and his voice sounded normal; he didn't seem ill. However, Greg still asked the man, "Do you have an upper respiratory problem?"

"Yes, I do. I have had it for over a week now, and I haven't been able to shake it."

Greg explained that I had received that impression for him and told him he needed to talk with me. The man took the phone, and I explained the impression I had received from God and told him that I believed it was an indication that God was near him and wanted to demonstrate that by healing him. I asked the man if I could pray for him and he agreed.

I prayed over the phone as Greg prayed in person with the man. Greg asked him if he felt anything as we were praying, and he said he did. He described how his symptoms were totally relieved and said, "I believe in that higher power stuff and spiritual cleansing."

Greg said, "Man, what you were feeling was Jesus."

The kingdom of God had shown up in the middle of the night while I was at home, my friend was working night shift, and the man was ending a night at the bar. The man started walking off, and then when he was about ten feet away from Greg, he turned and said, "Man, that feels good!"

Without having any language or theology to describe what had just happened, the man had been encountered by the reality of the kingdom of God at hand.

Having a Bad Day on Purpose

I was having one of those days. I was having a bad day, and I was having a bad day on purpose. The fact of the matter is that we all have choices. We may not be able to control the world around us, but we can control our attitude. This day, for reasons I can no longer remember, I decided to have a bad day— on purpose. I chose to wallow in my own self-pity and the more I wallowed, the worse my attitude got.

I was passing by a Vietnamese supermarket on my way home. I have a special love for imported sodas sold in this supermarket. My friend, Ed, and I had been visiting this store for a while, praying for the sick and occasionally seeing healings there. I thought a Vietnamese soda might help pick me up and get me back to my usual, cheerful self. I knew that it was going to take more than one soda to lift my mood, so I picked up a six pack.

I stood in line behind an older Asian gentleman. Out of nowhere, it seemed like his ear was being highlighted to me. I thought, *No way am I going to step out in faith and ask him if there is something wrong with his ear. He will probably tell me no, and this will only add insult to injury.* I was still in a bad mood, enjoying my wallowing.

Then my curiosity began to get the best of me. I began thinking, *What if this is God?* So I blurted out, "Hey man, is there something wrong with your ear?"

He turned around and mumbled something I could not understand, but it sounded like NO. I was embarrassed. All I wanted to do was to turn around immediately and head for the exit. But I had these sodas I still needed to pay for, so I chose to remain in line and die a slow death. My bad day was getting worse.

I knew the cashier behind the counter, as she owned the store. She began speaking to the older gentleman in Vietnamese. Then the man turned around pointing to one ear and then to the other saying, "Oh! This ear good, this ear hear no more!" Then it dawned on me that he had not understood me because he could only speak a little English.

The woman behind the counter became my translator so that I could more effectively minister to this man. He gave me permission to place my hand over his deaf ear. When I did, I prayed a short prayer, "Lord, open his ear."

To my surprise and unbelief he said, "Yes, I can hear!" I thought, *No way! It can't happen like this! This guy is pulling my leg. If this was really a healing, shouldn't there be more fireworks? It should take a lot longer than a few seconds to heal a deaf ear, right?*

I continued to question him to see if he was really healed. He continued to declare, "I can hear! I can hear!" I was still in doubt until he leaned over and said, "Do you do shoulders too? Now you pray for my shoulder. It is in pain."

I said, "Okay," and I prayed. Instantly, his shoulder was healed.

When I was through, I paid for my soda and walked out of the store shaking my head thinking, *"God, you are so good!"* God was doing something amazing for that man that day, but he was also doing something amazing in me. I was stuck in my self-centered wallowing, and by grace He allowed me to see what I was doing. He gave me the means of pulling out of it by allowing me to partner with Him to minister to someone else. That day I understood that the kingdom of God is at hand, even when you are having a bad day on purpose.

The Kingdom of God at Hand on Vacation

My friend, Shane Jason Mock, went with me to North Carolina to attend a conference. I felt that I was to really use this time as a vacation—a time to relax and retreat from ministry. I didn't want to get involved in any kind of evangelism or prophetic ministry out on the streets or in the conference while on this trip. I just wanted to take a few days to rest and allow God to minister to me.

Shane, on the other hand, was looking for every opportunity he could to demonstrate the reality of the kingdom. He was giving detailed prophetic words to people on the plane and in restaurants. He was excited to be practicing power evangelism, while all I wanted to do was be on vacation.

Shane had heard about a famous coffee roastery in a town we were passing through, and he was intent on finding it. Despite GPS and Internet directions, we could not find the location anywhere. Shane was getting really frustrated, so we stopped and asked someone for directions. We were told the coffee roastery had recently closed, so they suggested a different coffee shop to us. We ended up at a mediocre coffee shop, far out of the way from where we were heading. We were at a place would have never gone if it hadn't been for the unusual circumstances.

On our way in, I noticed three people sitting at a table outside the shop. They looked totally out of place, like they were homeless and disheveled. I couldn't help but feel compassion for them, and I began to sense impressions from God for them. I heard the impressions and wanted to ignore them. After all, this was my time to take a break from ministry.

We went into the coffee shop, but as we walked in, I found myself turning around and walking right back out toward the three people. Shane noticed what I was doing and, having known each other a long time and having ministered to others together, he knew immediately what was going on. He finished getting his order and then followed me outside.

I approached the two men and the woman asking, "Hey, excuse me. I know this sounds odd, but does one of you have a deaf right ear and pain in your left shoulder?" These were the two impressions that I thought I was hearing from God. They gave me the typical "what, are you crazy?!" look from them, so I repeated myself to give them a moment for the shock of my unexpected question to wear off.

After a moment of the awkward silence, one of the men eventually spoke up. "That's interesting..." Pointing to the other man, he said, "He is deaf in his right ear. I have pain in my shoulder, but you're wrong. It's in my right shoulder, not my left."

Pushing past my partial mistake in hearing God correctly, I asked him if I could pray for his shoulder, and he agreed to that. I prayed, after which he told me that he felt the pain leave.

I then turned to the other man and asked if I could pray for his hearing in his right ear to be healed. Having just seen his friend's shoulder healed, he agreed. We were all astonished as his hearing was miraculously restored after a very short prayer. We were testing it out by covering his good ear and whispering to him. He could hear incredibly well out of the ear that had been totally deaf moments before. His friends were completely amazed because they had known the severity of his hearing disability, and they were witnesses to the fact that he was hearing in a way that had been impossible before now.

These two healings opened a door for us to engage in conversation with these three people. They had experienced much brokenness and pain in their lives. One of them was carrying guilt and condemnation because of some criminal activity he had been involved in that resulted in the accidental death of his mother. We were able to share the gospel with the three of them, and they allowed us to speak into their lives in an incredible way. The lady opened up to us about her life, which enabled us to pray with her and help her through an inner healing process.

The amazing thing to me about this interaction was the divine providence of it all. I was totally not looking to do any ministry or evangelism that day. I was actually trying to avoid it. We were not even supposed to be at that coffee shop. God had orchestrated the events of that day to take us to an out-of-the-way, not-so-good coffee shop for one reason: because the kingdom of God was breaking into the lives of those three people. I realized that the kingdom of God is at hand even when you are on a vacation. His kingdom never stops advancing, and He desires for us to join Him in its advance.

Insight Five: We've Already Been Commissioned to Go

Our challenge is to stay focused on the mission of Christ in the world and our call to participate in that mission.

In the ninth chapter of Matthew, we see Jesus was ministering to many people, and His disciples were in tow. He healed a paralyzed man, healed a woman who had been hemorrhaging for years, raised a young girl from death, gave sight to two blind men, and topped it off by freeing a demonized mute, returning his speech. The chapter concludes with this:

> *Jesus went through all the towns and villages, teaching in their synagogues, proclaiming the good news of the kingdom and healing every disease and sickness. When he saw the crowds, he had compassion on them, because they were harassed and helpless, like sheep without a shepherd. Then he said to his disciples, "The harvest is plentiful but the workers are few. Ask the Lord of the harvest, therefore, to send out workers into his harvest field." (Matthew 9:35-38)*

As disciples of Jesus, these men had been following Him, listening to His teaching, and observing His miracles. They had witnessed Jesus' authority over sickness, disease, dangerous storms, and even death. Then they joined Jesus in this fervent prayer: "Lord, send laborers into the harvest!"

I wonder if they anticipated what happened next. I wonder if they understood the implications of this prayer. In the very next verse, we see a critical change in Jesus' ministry strategy. Instead of heading out to the next town and ministering as He had been doing, Matthew 10:1 says,

> *He called his twelve disciples to him and gave them authority to drive out evil spirits and to heal every disease and sickness... These twelve Jesus sent out with the following instructions: Go to the lost sheep of Israel. As you go, preach this message: "The kingdom of heaven has come near." Heal the sick, raise the dead, cleanse those who have leprosy, drive out demons. Freely you have received, freely give. (Matthew 10:1,5-6)*

Suddenly, Jesus' message became their message. Jesus' authority was now their authority. Jesus' mission was now their mission. We see later in Luke 10 that Jesus similarly sent out seventy-two other nameless disciples with the same authority and instruction. It was clear that Jesus did not intend for ministry to be confined to Himself. He freely passed it on to His followers.

Among the truly amazing dynamics about Jesus' approach to ministry is that He did it in such a way that it could be duplicated in the lives of His disciples. These earliest disciples were simply laborers and businessmen from the community. Jesus did His ministry in His humanity empowered by the Holy Spirit. Miracles did not simply attest to Jesus' divinity, they attested to His radical dependence on the Holy Spirit. The early followers of Jesus understood that discipleship meant more than being familiar with Jesus' teaching; they were to engage in His ministry as well. This was true for the early followers of Christ, but what about those who continue to follow Him two thousand years later?

As disciples today, we are given the exact same instructions by the same Jesus who commissioned the original twelve.

As you go, preach this message: "The kingdom of heaven has come near." Heal the sick, raise the dead, cleanse those who have leprosy, drive out demons. Freely you have received, freely give. (Matthew 10:7-8)

Because of the goodness of God, we have received freely from the cup of God's grace. We have partaken of the saving power of the risen and ruling Lord Jesus. What we have freely received we are to freely give away.

A disciple is someone who emulates his teacher. He learns from and apprentices under the teacher with the goal of becoming like him. Our teacher, Jesus, went about healing the sick, forgiving sinners, driving out demons, showing compassion to the marginalized, and raising the dead. As disciples, our lives are to be marked by the same.

Jesus trained His disciples to operate in signs and wonders. Certainly this was not something that was on the regular resume of a fisherman or a tax collector; nonetheless, Jesus expected His disciples to learn the art of operating in the realm of the Spirit. His goal was to develop them into the type of people who could advance the kingdom of God. The proclamation and demonstration of the kingdom of God involved healing the sick, casting out demons, and raising the dead. These skills were something the disciples had to learn. They had to learn to have the type of faith that resulted in miracles, and the gospel record is clear that they did not learn without some bumps in the road. They often failed or gave up in frustration (see Matthew 17:14-20). They commonly ministered with impure motives (see Mark 9:33-34). Jesus didn't feel the need to wait for them to be perfect to begin ministry. He used ministry as a means to refine them into people who not only partnered in His mission, but also reflected His character.

Like the disciples, we too must develop new ways of thinking and new abilities in order to operate in the gifts of the Spirit. It does not come naturally to us either. The process of learning from Jesus to operate in signs and wonders is one that will involve trial and error, and likely, frequent failures also. Just like the disciples, there may be times when we will fail and want to give up. There are times when our motives will not be right or our faith will be lacking. We must not use those occasions as excuses to stop doing the ministry of Jesus, but rather as springboards into a deeper relationship with Christ, allowing Him to refine us and shape us more and more into His image.

The Great Commission

Many of us are familiar with the Great Commission found in Matthew 28:18-20:

> *All authority in heaven and on earth has been given to me. Therefore, go and make disciples of all nations, baptizing them in the name of the Father and of the Son and of the Holy Spirit, and teaching them to obey everything I have commanded you. And surely I am with you always, to the very end of the age.*

We have already been commissioned to continue the mission of Christ in the world. This would seem to be a daunting task if not for two important facts. The first is that the gospel itself has intrinsic power. The apostle Paul writes, "I am not ashamed of the gospel, because it is the power of God for the salvation of everyone who believes" (Romans 1:16). We are not proclaiming our ideas or thoughts; we are declaring God's good news. There is power in the message.

Second, the Holy Spirit empowers us. In Jesus' post-resurrection appearances to His disciples, He instructed them to "wait for the gift my Father promised" and "you will receive power when the Holy Spirit comes on you; and you will be my witnesses" (Acts 1:4,8). The apostle Paul tells us to be "filled with the Spirit" (Ephesians 5:18). The presence and power of the Holy Spirit is available to us for the asking. It is as simple as taking a few moments during the day to slow down and simply ask God to fill us with His presence. His presence brings insight, strength, wisdom, and supernatural power.

As commissioned ones, we are to carry out Jesus' ministry by being disciples who reproduce ourselves by making disciples of others. We need not wait on some mystical sign from heaven that we have been called to participate in the ministry of Christ. We don't need to wait until we have the right impartation from the right person in the right way. Jesus already supplied this for us two thousand years ago. He will sometimes grace us with faith by assuring us of our mission or bringing clarity concerning how we are to walk it out. We should not diminish the weight of what Jesus was imparting when He said "All authority in heaven and on earth has been given to me. Therefore, go!"

As we go, we are encouraged because Jesus doesn't simply equip us and then send us out on our own. He promises to go with us. "And surely I am with you always, to the very end of the age" (Matthew 28:20).

As You Go...

Remember the passage in Matthew 10 when Jesus first sent out the disciples with His authority? Jesus said,

> As you go, proclaim this message: 'The kingdom of heaven has come near.' Heal the sick, raise the dead, cleanse those who have leprosy, drive out demons. (Matthew 10:7-8)

Many of us are waiting for God to bring us into a special time and place in which we will begin/do our ministry. We think that God has a special calling for us which will be this amazing thing outside of our everyday mundane reality. The truth is that Jesus empowered His disciples to carry out the mission of the kingdom "as you go."

It is a profound mistake many Christians make to compartmentalize their lives: family time, work time, Jesus time, and ministry time. If we continue to look for some elusive setting or situation in which to begin partnering with Jesus in His mission, then we will never find it. We will find it "as you go." It is in the midst of our everyday lives that we find ourselves at the intersection of a person whom God loves, our seemingly unimpressive routine, and God's divine plan. Because Jesus has already given us authority and commissioned us to go, we should expect that He will bring the people along our path to whom He desires to demonstrate His love. We don't need to wait to go on the mission field to evangelize the lost and heal the sick—we can do it from our desk at work, during our stroll through Walmart, while drinking coffee at Starbucks, at our dinner tables, or wherever we find ourselves in our normal lives.

One of our favorite scriptures is Acts 10:38:

God anointed Jesus of Nazareth with the Holy Spirit and power, and he went around doing good and healing all who were under the power of the devil, because God was with him.

Jesus walked in power, healing, signs, and wonders as "He went around." Likewise, as we make our way through life, we are also anointed with the same Holy Spirit and power to do good, healing all who are under the power of the devil, because God is with us.

As we learn to take seriously the Great Commission, it will become more and more normal for power encounters to happen as we go through our day-to-day lives. We have learned to integrate evangelism into our daily lives as we go. We look for opportunities to partner with the Holy Spirit in the grocery store, with a waiter at a restaurant, on the phone with a client, and with anyone else we may encounter "as we go."

SuperHealing at SuperCuts

Have you ever had one of those bad hair days and nothing you seemed to do would fix it? It happened to be one of those days. In fact, my hair was so bad I (Brian) looked in the mirror, and all I could see were those late-night commercials flashing through my head: "Ch-ch-ch-chia pet." So I threw on a hat and headed to my favorite place to get my hair cut only to find out that the lady who usually cuts my hair wasn't in, and there wouldn't be anyone else to cut my hair for a couple of hours. I was incredibly frustrated. So, because the need was dire, I went to SuperCuts. I walked in and saw three ladies cutting hair. I was thinking to myself, *I would like that lady, or that lady, but I don't want* her *touching my hair.* I was judging that lady by her appearance. Of course, it was that lady who called my name to cut my hair.

As I was sitting in the chair, I started seeing a picture in my mind of a stomach and an ulcer. I felt like the Lord was saying the lady has an ulcer in her stomach and Jesus wanted to touch her. I had a choice: *Am I going to share this word with the lady, or am I going to hold it and never see if it is the Lord?* Then I had to decide when I would share the word. *Should I go ahead and do it now? Should I wait until she's done cutting my hair? What about the awkward silence if I'm wrong? What if I'm right? Would she become totally undone and mess up my hair?*

I waited till she was almost done and said, "Excuse me, ma'am, but sometimes I get pictures and impressions for people. Do you mind if I share what I got with you?" She gave me a *what kind of a weirdo are you!* look. I explained to her, "I saw a stomach with an ulcer. By any chance do you have an ulcer in your stomach?"

She began to weep and cry, "How did you know? This is weird! I have goose bumps all over! How did you know this?"

I said to her, "I didn't know this, but Jesus did, and He wants to encounter you with His love. Do you mind if I pray for you after you finish with my hair? I believe Jesus wants to heal you." I asked her where she wanted me to pray for her, and she directed me to the back room.

I told her I was just going to pray and ask Jesus to touch her, and I asked if that was OK. She said yes. As I began to pray for her, she began to shake all over. I don't know if that's something that normally happens in SuperCuts or not, but it was what was happening that day. I asked her what she was feeling, and she said she was hot all over her body. I explained that what she was feeling was the presence of God coming to touch her body.

Suddenly, I felt an electrical shock run through my body, and I did a weird, involuntary jerking gesture. I apologized: "I'm sorry—I don't understand that. Sometimes that happens to me when the power of God is present."

She seemed a little nervous, so I asked her to put her hand on her own stomach. I said, "Holy Spirit, come," and the Lord began touching her even more.

She was shouting, "Oh my gosh! Oh my gosh! I feel this heat and tingling rushing into my stomach!"

"I guess Jesus has come to touch you today. I should probably get my ticket and go now." And that's how I left it. Jesus came and wanted to encounter this lady. I was in an attitude of frustration and judgment, but in that moment I heard the voice of God break in on behalf of that lady.

God empowers us at the point of someone else's need. This means that we must intentionally move toward ministry opportunities where we are totally in over our heads. Rather than hiding from the sick and the lost, we are to move toward them with the confidence that the kingdom of God is at hand. God loves them, He is active in their lives, and the Holy Spirit will empower us with what He wants us to minister in the moment of need. We don't have to look far and wide for people to minister to. God is involved in the lives of everyone around us. We simply partner with what God is doing "as we go."

Jesus Walked Into a Sushi Bar

Our friend, Shane Jason Mock, lives his life by two mottos: "doing life with God" and "live a life of intimacy and impact." He has truly integrated the value of living out the commission of Christ into every area of his life, from the extraordinary to the mundane. As we live a life of intimacy with the Father, we have greater impact in fulfilling our commission to love people and encounter them with His love. Here is one of Shane's stories:

> We had just finished a couple of hours of ministry at church and I felt exhausted. Brian was craving sushi, so Brian, his wife Jeanine, and I headed for a sushi restaurant. When we walked into the restaurant I felt my exhaustion leaving and renewed energy coming into my body. Many times when the presence of the Holy Spirit

comes on me for ministry I feel a sense of energy and warmth on my body.

When our waitress, Jen, came to take our drink orders, I said, "There is this entrepreneurial calling that's all over your life. I don't know if it's happened yet, but you are going to be starting a business. When that time comes, don't be afraid to take the risk, because it really is part of your destiny."

"Oh my God, oh my God, oh my God!" she replied, clutching her chest for breath. "You are really freaking me out here."

"How so?" I asked.

"I have been thinking for some time about starting a restaurant. Two months ago, I went ahead and got the papers for the loan from the bank. Last week, I threw away the papers, because I just couldn't see how the money was going to work out," she replied, still shaking her head.

I told her, "Well, I would encourage you to rethink that decision, because I believe that this is God's heart for you."

I tried ordering again, but she continued, "This is so freaky. I was just looking at those papers."

Brian piped in, "Pretty crazy stuff, huh?"

Our waitress left to the kitchen, bewildered. This was one of those occasions where I did not feel a need to rush anything. I knew she had to come back to get our orders and she was obviously touched in a deep way. I was certain that we were likely to have the opportunity to have additional interaction on a spiritual level. I have found that people are longing to have spiritual conversations and they are willing to listen after being touched by Jesus. Proclamation typically follows demonstration, or to quote John Wimber, "The kingdom involves both show and tell."

Brian and Jeanine ordered stir-fry, so a Ginsu chef came to prepare the meal. The chef was personable and seemed to be really open to us. Throughout the food preparation, he told us about his family and his spiritual journey. It was evident that he wasn't open to "organized religion."

As we neared the end of the food preparation, I began to share some impressions I had. When the Holy Spirit speaks to me it often feels like a conversation I had two or three weeks ago; it feels like an almost forgotten memory on which I have to focus to recall some of the details. Speaking to our chef, I tried to use non-church language. "I have the impression that you have a real strong networking gift. As part of that networking gift, you are going to be bringing together groups of people and creating a feeling of community. This community is going to be a support system to many, and it is going to function like family in the way it supports people." I continued, "Also, totally unrelated to that, I see you coaching basketball. I don't know if that's something that has already happened, or it it's going to be happening, but there is going to be this opportunity to coach basketball."

I was glad that most of our food was done cooking, because his attention was no longer on the food. "So, you're psychic?" he asked.

Brian jumped in, "Well, he's a Christian psychic." Brian and I have found it helpful when ministering to non-Christians to use terms and categories that people are familiar with rather than getting bogged down in correcting these kinds of misunderstandings. Even Daniel in the Old Testament was called, "chief of the magicians."

"That's crazy, man. I was in the back and Jen told me about you. She was blown away. Now I understand. My friend is a basketball coach at one of the local high schools. Last week, he called me to shoot some hoops. While I was there he asked me to consider becoming an assistant coach."

"Where do you go to church?" the chef asked. I told him. I could see the wheels in his mind turning. He went back to the kitchen.

Jen returned a short time later, and after asking us if we wanted dessert, she blurted out, "Who are you? What is this about?" I began sharing my story of how I came to know Jesus in a personal way and His desire to be in our lives in a real and tangible way. She responded, sharing some of her spiritual journey as well. None of it involved Jesus.

As she was talking, I felt God give me more insight into her life, so I added, "I also see a lot of late-night phone calls. There is this gift of counsel that's coming upon you. Your friends in troubled situations are going to be calling you. In fact they are going to be sleeping on your couch."

"Oh my God! This is crazy! This is so right on," she exclaimed. Turning to Brian, she asked, "Are you one?"

"What do you mean?" Brian asked.

"One of the…" she paused, "weird ones."

Before Brian had a chance to answer, I interjected that Brian has seen God heal many people over the years. Without missing a beat, Brian said, "Do you want to see something really wild?"

"I don't know," she said. "I don't know if I can take any more of this."

Brian told her to hold out her hands as if she were going to receive a gift. She opened her hands, asking, "What are you going to do to me?" Brian responded by telling her that he was going to ask God to pour out His love on her and touch her physically.

When Brian began praying, she exclaimed, "What are you doing to me! Oh my God, oh my God, oh my God. I feel heat and goose bumps from my stomach flowing all through my body. You have to stop. This is freaking me out!"

Brain asked her, "Are you having pain in your lower back?"

The waitress replied, "Yes, oh my God, this is crazy."

Brian continued, "Are you having trouble sleeping, too?" She replied yes. Brian prayed that God would relieve her pain and enable her to sleep.

Brian then told her to move around and see if the pain had left. She began stretching side to side, shaking her head in disbelief, saying, "There is no pain." Brian encouraged her to ask God to continue to visit her when she went to bed that night.

To cap off our dinner, we left a large tip. If you are going to do the work of the kingdom in a restaurant, it's important to tip very well. We left. Nobody prayed the sinner's prayer. We did not leave a tract or get any follow up information. We simply did what we believed Jesus wanted us to do in the moment. But I think we left enough puzzle pieces that the sushi staff could begin to interact with Jesus and His community if they wanted to.

While it's true that this is not necessarily the norm for most times when we go to restaurants, it is also true that these types of experiences have become common for me. As we understand the gravity of what Jesus already imparted to us when He gave us authority to carry out His ministry and mission, we become more and more aware of God's heart for those around us everywhere we go. The more we sense and share in the compassion of Jesus for the people we encounter in our daily lives, the more we are in a position to minister the love of Christ to them.

Insight Six: Develop the Art of Seeing, Hearing, and Doing

Our challenge is to expectantly watch for God's activity, listen to His voice and discern His will in the present moment.

Jesus Does What He Sees the Father Doing

Jesus' earthly ministry was characterized by healings, miracles, deliverances, and the proclamation of truth. Jesus' actions were a reflection of the heart of the Father for His children. In John 14:9, Jesus said that anyone who had seen Him had seen the Father. In Colossians 1:15, Paul described Jesus as the image of the invisible God. What the Father was doing in heaven, Jesus was doing on earth. The Father's will in heaven was being made manifest on earth in the words and actions of Jesus. In John 14:10, Jesus stated, "The words I say to you are not just my own. Rather, it is the Father, living in me, who is doing his work."

Jesus viewed His ministry as that of simply doing what He saw the Father already doing. John 5:19-20 says:

> *Jesus gave them this answer: "I tell you the truth, the Son can do nothing by himself; he can do only what he sees his Father doing, because whatever the Father does the Son also does. For the Father loves the Son and shows him all he does."*

Jesus healed the sick, cleansed the lepers, and raised the dead because it was what He saw the Father doing. If the Father was doing it, the Son was also doing it. If the Father wasn't doing it, the Son didn't do it. It was out of their love relationship that the Father showed Jesus all He was doing. Love paved the way for insight into the Father's activities. Out of His intimate relationship with the Father, Jesus was able to see and hear what the Father was doing. Once He saw and heard, He joined the Father in these activities.

Jesus calls us to do ministry in the same way. In John 14:12, Jesus declared:

> I tell you the truth, anyone who has faith in me will do what I have been doing. He will do even greater things than these, because I am going to the Father.

With the ascension of Jesus and the coming of the Holy Spirit, we are now entrusted with the ministry of Jesus. Now we are the ones who are to do what we see the Father doing and say what we hear the Father saying. We are to reflect the activities of heaven here on earth. Because the Father loves us and He loves those we encounter, He will show us what He is doing. Our job is to learn to see, hear, and do the Father's work here on earth.

This concept can seem daunting, especially to those of us whose worldview makes it difficult to believe that we can actually see, hear, and do the works of the Father. The good news is that we can develop the art of seeing, hearing, and doing. It will require lots of trust, and it will involve taking risks. We will likely fail more times than we succeed, but the successes are worth the risk because it means a little more of heaven has come to earth. We are powerless to do anything without the aid of the Holy Spirit, and we must lean on Him as we endeavor to see, hear, and do the works of the Father.

Two Favorite Prayers

When we find ourselves face to face with a sick person, we have no healing to give them. When praying for a demonized individual, there is no deliverance dust we have to sprinkle on them. When praying for someone in need of a miracle or prophetic word, we cannot reach into our pockets and pull one out. However, the Holy Spirit has everything that is needed. It doesn't matter if you think you have a healing gift or not—the Holy Spirit does. It doesn't matter if you are evangelist or not—the Holy Spirit is.

John Wimber taught two very short, powerful, and effective prayers we have learned to pray when we step into a situation that requires supernatural intervention. The first is *"Help!!"* The second is *"O God, o God, o God!!"* Outwardly we may look calm and assured, but in our hearts we know that if God does not empower us with His presence in the moments of need, then not much is going to happen. We may not pray these two prayers out loud, but they are welling up within us as we look to God for the power we need.

Sometimes we have an idea beforehand of what God wants to do, and every now and then we may even have a sense of anointing; but most of the time we don't feel anything at all. We simply pray for others out of obedience to Christ and His Word. He told us to pray for the sick, so when someone needs prayer, regardless of how we feel, we believe it is our responsibility and privilege to pray.

In Luke 11, the disciples asked Jesus how to pray. He taught them the Lord's Prayer and concluded the discussion with these encouraging words:

> *Which of you fathers, if your son asks for a fish, will give him a snake instead? Or if he asks for an egg, will give*

him a scorpion? If you then, though you are evil, know how to give good gifts to your children, how much more will your Father in heaven give the Holy Spirit to those who ask him! (Luke 11:11-13)

Jesus has promised us that when we ask for the Holy Spirit, He will give us the Holy Spirit. This is great news, mostly because we have nothing else to offer the people we are ministering to. No matter how practiced and refined we are in the art of evangelism, we can still do absolutely nothing without the working of the Holy Spirit upon the person.

All the gifts of the Spirit are resident in the Holy Spirit, so when He comes, all the gifts come with Him. He empowers us, in that instant, with what He wants to give us. We can only give to others what He gives to us at the moment of prayer. We don't carry any extra healing virtue on our persons; neither do we have any extra prophetic ministry or words of wisdom. As His disciples, we only have His ministry. We are totally dependent on the Holy Spirit and what He gives us in the moment. Practically speaking, what this means is that God is equally, lovingly working in both us and the person we are ministering to.

Spiritual Gifts

Many times Christians approach spiritual gifts as something separate from the person and activity of the Holy Spirit. It is not as if God gives us a spiritual gift and then steps back and watches to see what we will do with it. Spiritual gifts are not simply spiritual objects, tools, or even manifestations; they are simply a title or tag to define the activity we are doing with the Holy Spirit. Empowered ministry is always active partnership with God. Fundamental to effective empowered ministry is intimacy with the Holy Spirit.

The New Testament epistles list specific spiritual gifts in a number of different passages (1 Corinthians 12:28, 1 Corinthians 12:8-10, Ephesians 4:11, Romans 12:6-8, 1 Peter 4:11). What is interesting is that each list is different. This seems to indicate that Paul and Peter were not attempting to compile an exhaustive list of spiritual gifts but were instead citing various examples of spiritual gifts.

As a Christian, there have been times when you have been led and empowered by the Holy Spirit. You have operated in the use of spiritual gifts whether you were aware of it or not. In fact, it has been our experience that regardless of your theological understanding in relationship to spiritual gifts, as a Christian seeking to follow Jesus and minster to others, the Holy Spirit is already empowering you.

People often approach the gifts of the Spirit in one of two ways. One perspective places the emphasis on the gifted person—that an individual has a certain spiritual gift. For example, Philip is called an evangelist (Acts 21:8); Judas and Silas are called prophets (Acts 15:32); so there are clearly people who have manifestations of certain gifts to the extent that they are known to carry those giftings. There are people today who walk in the office of prophet, evangelist, or healer. While this is a clearly biblical approach to spiritual gifts, the mistake many Christians make is to conclude that because they are not one of these specially gifted individuals, they cannot learn and grow in the exercise of spiritual gifts.

The second way to view spiritual gifts is that the gifts belong to the Holy Spirit and He gives them situationally as they are needed. When we encounter people who need healing, then the Holy Spirit is the One who will provide a gift of healing. If they need wisdom, the Holy Spirit will provide a word of wisdom, and so on. The Spirit chooses to accomplish these activities through the church—through ordinary Christians like you and me. Therefore, whether we consider ourselves to be gifted in a certain area or not, the Holy Spirit can use us to minister to a person with whatever gift is needed at that time.

Paul certainly believed all followers of Jesus could grow in spiritual gifts. Although he taught that the gifts are given at the Holy Spirit's discretion, he also encouraged us to ask for them. Paul tells the church to "Follow the way of love and eagerly desire spiritual gifts, especially prophecy" (1 Corinthians 14:1, see also 1 Corinthians 12:31, 14:39). Love and Spirit-empowered ministry are to go hand in hand.

Because Paul instructs us to eagerly desire spiritual gifts, we can be certain that all the gifts are attainable and accessible to the believer at the point of another person's need for them. Furthermore, Paul later tells Timothy to "fan into flame the gift of God which is in you" (2 Timothy 1:6). Clearly, there is responsibility on our part to grow in the gifts of God so that we can become more effective in ministry.

While these two approaches to spiritual gifts may initially seem at odds with each other, in reality both are equally true. Whether or not you feel you are gifted in healing or prophecy or any other gift, the Holy Spirit can gift you with the manifestation of these gifts in situations where they are needed. If you are with someone in need of healing, you need not wait for a person gifted in healing to arrive on the scene. The same Holy Spirit who gifts those with a more recognized ministry of healing (in the sense that God uses them to heal on a fairly frequent basis) can equally gift you in that situation. After all, the gift is not for you. It is for the person in need and for the glory of the Father.

Empowered ministry is an activity of the Holy Spirit and, ultimately, it is the Holy Spirit who empowers us to minister. It has been our experience that the Holy Spirit gives us the grace to minister as we actually engage in ministry. It would be great if we always felt some sense of gifting or empowerment before we began praying for a person, but in our experience this rarely happens. We have discovered that it is as we step out in faith that spiritual gifts are imparted and demonstrated.

The ability to discern God's activity is like learning a second language: we can hear the words but we don't yet understand the message; but it can, in fact, be learned. This comes as a surprise to many people. They believe that if it's God at work then His message should be clear, but this is not always the case. Proverbs 25:2 says, "It is the glory of God to conceal a matter; to search out a matter is the glory of kings." Sometimes God intentionally conceals His activity in order for us to seek Him and search it out. The amazing thing is that He not only wants to speak to us and work through us, but He does it in such a way that it causes us to press deeper into relationship with Him.

Jesus frequently spoke to people in parables, knowing that many people would not understand the truth He was communicating. On many occasions, Jesus had to explain the meaning of His parables to His disciples. Likewise, we must learn the language that God is speaking to us in order to minister effectively to the people around us. This is a process that requires patience, risk, and a desire to deepen our intimacy with God. In order to discern God's activity, one must become teachable and willing to take chances.

When I (Brian) was still quite new to hearing the voice of God for others, I had an alarming vision which illustrates this point. I was at a home group meeting, and we were entering into prayer time. A mental picture popped into my mind. The image I saw was a naked lady in a shower. I thought, *Oh my gosh! What's wrong with me? What a pervert! I can't believe I'm having lust issues during a time of prayer.* I was trying to repent and shut the image out of my mind when I remembered something Charles had taught me: if you see a strange or alarming picture during a time a prayer, ask the Father, "What are you saying to me in this image?" Then all of a sudden I saw the scene again. No matter how hard the woman tried to scrub herself, she never felt clean. I shared the vision with the group, and as I did several women began to weep and say that the vision was about them. God was able to do some deep healing in several women that day. God was speaking to me in symbolic language, and I had to seek Him to find out what He was doing in that situation.

Learning to Discern God's Voice and Activity

Intentionally discerning the activity of God is a learned skill and the activation of His supernatural power is usually at the moment of need. We can learn to see, hear, feel, and think what God is doing.

When we train people to see and hear what God is doing, it is not unusual for them to tell us that they have been seeing and hearing the same kinds of things for many years, but they were not aware God was speaking to them. They have been having visions or feeling impressions, but they have never had the language or context to explain the experiences, so they unconsciously dismissed them rather than sought God to discern what He was saying and showing them.

Discerning the voice of God involves three parts: revelation, interpretation, and application. As you practice hearing the voice of God and responding to it, you will become better and better at integrating all three.

Revelation is receiving the "raw data" from God. This is information that God is downloading. This data is what we see, hear, feel, and think. God is speaking to us all the time, but we need to take the time to wait and listen and then to process what He may be saying.

It is important to note that revelation is often very faint and very fleeting. It would be nice if God made a habit of creating neon signs in the sky or speaking audibly to us. While He does at times speak to us in undeniable and dramatic ways, this is almost always the exception to the rule. As Elijah discovered, God often speaks to us in a still, small voice.

Revelation can come in infinite ways because we serve an infinite God with infinite creativity, but we have narrowed down the following possibilities to most common ways God speaks to us today:

- You can see it.
- You can hear it.
- You can feel it.
- You can think it.

This can also be called operating in the gift of word of knowledge (see 1 Corinthians 12:8). A word of knowledge is information which God gives about a person or situation that we could not have known on our own.

See It: This can be something as simple as a mental picture which pops in your mind as you are praying. The picture may symbolize something God wants to communicate. Jesus said He only did what He saw the Father doing. In Habakkuk 2:1-2 the writer records, "I will look to see what He will say to me... Then the Lord replied: 'Write down the revelation.'" Habakkuk equated hearing from God with seeing a vision.

There are also times when you are in prayer and you see pictures of parts of people's bodies or organs in your mind. This may be an indication of God's desire to heal those areas in a person's body. As you learn to relax and wait on God, you may find that He will often give an image or a picture in your mind's eye.

On occasion, someone may be highlighted to you. You find yourself drawn to them. When we teach people how to do power evangelism on the streets, we ask them to look around and see who they might be drawn to. Then we ask them to ask God to give them supernatural insight into the person they are looking at. We then instruct them to share (in a non-religious way) what they think they heard from the Lord and to use that as a springboard into sharing about the love of God.

Other times you may catch a glimpse of something with your natural eyes, such as a shadow, bright light, or anything unusual that grabs your attention. Many times God is speaking to you through the visual things you are drawn to.

Hear It: You may hear an internal, audible voice in your mind. In Scripture, the phrase, "The word of the Lord came to me saying…" probably refers to the internal audible voice. Most often it will sound like your thoughts, but it is coming from a source other than your own imagination. This type of hearing is very common and we often dismiss it because it sounds just like our own internal voice. Our thoughts can usually be traced; we have a train of thought. If what you just heard seemed totally random—you can't connect it to the train of thought you had before—then it may be God's voice interrupting your train of thought. The only way to know if it is God or just your imagination is to just step out and share what you think you heard.

At other times you may hear an audible voice with your ears, but no one else does, even though someone might be standing next to you. Samuel heard his name being called so loudly that he thought it might be Eli, but Eli did not hear it (1 Samuel 3:1-14). This audible type of hearing is much less common than internal hearing. While it would be great for God to always speak to us audibly, we must learn to tune our ears to hear and discern the internal voice of God as well.

Feel It: There are times when we feel a "sympathetic pain" in or on our body that may indicate where someone else is hurting. Sometimes these sympathetic pains are fleeting, other times they may be quite intense. For example, if you suddenly get a random pain in your knee without any apparent cause, it may not be *your* knee at all. It may be a word of knowledge for healing for a person around you who has knee pain. This is a concept quite foreign to our western view of reality, so it takes practice to stop owning every sensation in our physical bodies and realize sometimes God may be speaking to us about things He desires to do for others through our bodies.

Our bodies sometimes also sense the presence and activity of God. It may feel like a sense of peace or empowerment. This can manifest as heat or tingling in our bodies, slight or considerable trembling.

There are times when God may allow you to feel the emotions others are feeling. These feelings can be recognized as the emotions of others because they are generally foreign to what you would normally feel in that situation. These feelings are not our own but are a word of knowledge from the Lord about someone else's feelings. It is an indication of what God is doing at that time in the life of someone else. It is often an invitation to enter into those emotions with that person as a means of providing empathetic comfort to them in their time of emotional need. Other times it is simply an invitation to pray for the person.

The first time I (Charles) became consciously aware of this type of revelation from the Lord was before a church service several years ago. I was in prayer, asking God what He wanted to do during the service. I was immediately filled with a tremendous sadness. When I asked God what this meant, I saw a mental picture of about a half dozen faces, some of which I did not recognize. My interpretation was that these were people God wanted to pour out His love on that morning.

After the worship portion of our service, I got up and described what I felt in prayer and invited anyone who fit that description to come up for prayer. Everyone I saw in prayer came up for ministry. I would never have known to pray for healing over sadness if I hadn't responded to the feeling of sadness I experienced earlier that morning in prayer. By recognizing that this feeling was a word of knowledge for someone else and acting on this impression, many people were touched by the love of God that morning.

Think It: This is simply something you know. There is no rational reason for how you know. You just think you know something to be true and you don't know why. When Jesus was talking to the woman at the well, He knew she had five husbands and was not married to the man with whom she was living (John 4:1-30). On other occasions, Scripture simply says Jesus knew someone's thoughts or plans (Matthew 22:18, Mark 2:8, John 6:15).

Sometimes these impressions are quite clear, other times they are less certain. They are a sense that we ought to do something or that something might be true. God uses impressions or feelings to guide us. Nehemiah said, "So my God put it into my heart to assemble the nobles..." (Nehemiah 7:5). These knowings and impressions do not come from a detailed thought process; they are usually spontaneous and not premeditated.

Most of the time, revelation is fleeting. You think you might have heard something or seen something, and it is gone as quickly and faintly as it came. If you try to recreate the words or see the vision again it seems illusive. This doesn't mean it wasn't real. Learn to capture the fleeting impressions and just step out in faith. If you're wrong, you're wrong. Worst case scenario, you have learned more about hearing the voice of God through your mistake. Best case scenario, you still learn more about hearing the voice of God, and the person to whom you are ministering receives a divine touch from the Lord and walks away changed.

Quite often when revelation comes to us, it doesn't carry any meaning with it. For example, you may have an impression about horses, but it doesn't mean anything to you. This is where we press into the next step of the process by asking God for the interpretation of what He is saying to us.

Interpretation is the process of discerning what God is trying to tell us through revelation. It is not enough to hear God speak; we must take the time to ask God what the revelation means. Even If the revelation is accurate, it is still possible to get a wrong interpretation. It was not unusual for Jesus to have to explain His parables to His disciples. It should not surprise us that Jesus must do the same with us.

If you get an impression or revelation, take a moment to pause and ask God, "What are you saying to me about that? What are you doing in that?" This type of dialogue with God is critical for gaining understanding and arriving at a correct interpretation. We see an example of this type of dialogue in the Bible going on between Amos and the Lord when Amos was getting the vision of the plumb line. It was through a back-and-forth dialogue with the Father that Amos received full understanding (see Amos 7).

There may be times when you ask the Father for interpretation and you don't get anything. It's okay to ask the person you are praying for if it is meaningful to them. Sometimes they will have the interpretation.

A number of years ago, I (Charles) was praying for an older woman and received an impression of an orange. When I asked the Lord what this meant, I did not receive anything from God, so I asked the woman if this image meant anything to her. She told me no, so I told her, "Let's ask the Lord what this means." Both of us came up blank and I began to feel a little desperate. I had been doing this long enough to know that the image must mean something but was surprised when we both seemed to draw a blank.

I then asked her if she was allergic to oranges. She said yes, that eating any kind of citrus fruit caused an allergic reaction. My sense (and hope) was that God might want to heal her, so we prayed for physical healing. A week later I received a telephone call from her pastor telling me that she bought an orange on the way home that evening and there was no allergic reaction, and she had been eating oranges all week since then.

You can receive a true revelation from God, but if you misinterpret it, the ministry time may prove to be ineffective. It is important that you keep a humble posture and stay away from religious language such as "The Lord showed me...." or "Thus says the Lord..." It is much more effective to say "I have an impression" (which is true), "does this make any sense to you?"

In time, you may discover that God will give you a language of symbols, pictures, and feelings unique to you that will help you interpret what your are receiving.

Even if you receive correct revelation and interpretation about what God is speaking to you, it is important to remember that there is a reason why God is speaking to you—it needs to be applied. Application is the final step in receiving and responding to a word from God.

Application is what you do with the revelation and interpretation. Once you have received a sense of what God is saying or doing, it is important to ask God to show you what to do with what He has given you. Sometimes God simply wants you to intercede for the person in private; other times He may want you to share or act on what He has shown you.

For example, maybe God is speaking to you about the person you are ministering to needing to forgive someone else. Sharing this understanding with him has some intrinsic value, but much greater healing will come as you pray with that person and walk him through the forgiveness process.

Application is simply doing what God is asking us to do and responding to His leading. For example, let's say God gives you a picture of a shoulder, and you interpret this as meaning the person you're praying for or talking to has a shoulder condition which Jesus wants to heal. So far, so good, but it's only as you apply this understanding by stepping out to pray for the person's shoulder to be healed that the kingdom actually comes this person's life.

A true revelation with a correct interpretation but with the wrong application can cause the ministry to be ineffective. Our aim is always to show God's love and partner with God in ministering His purposes. Even if we get our wires crossed and somehow minister ineffectively, we can always demonstrate love. Regardless of what happens during the prayer time, the person receiving prayer should always feel loved by God and loved by you.

P's for Pursuing Power Ministry

So how do we grow in operating in spiritual gifts? There are many aspects involved in growing in the gifts. It is a divine partnership between the Holy Spirit and us as we yield to His activity in our lives. Below are some "P's" we have discovered as ways to help us grow in the gifts, particularly in the power gifts, such as healing and prophecy.

1. Pray

All effective ministry we do is in partnership with the Father by the empowerment of the Holy Spirit, so it must begin and end with prayer. We pray and ask the Holy Spirit to give His gifts, for they are His to distribute to each person as He wills (1 Corinthians 12:11). Paul encourages the believers in Corinth to pray for spiritual gifts and eagerly desire them (1 Corinthians 14:1, 14:13, 14:39). Likewise, we are to seek the Lord for spiritual gifts. It is in prayer that we ask for the gifts and we listen as the Lord guides and instructs us.

In Luke 11:5-13, Jesus shares a parable about someone who comes to you at night in need of food though you have none. We go to a friend who does have food to ask him for help, and we boldly continue to ask for food on behalf of this other person. Because of our persistence and boldness, our friend gives us the food.

This is a symbolic picture of ministry. We have nothing to give the people we are ministering to, but as we boldly and persistently go to our Friend who has all the food, we will be given what we need. Jesus concludes this parable by saying that when we ask for the Holy Spirit we will be given the Holy Spirit. In other words, we have nothing to give people other than what the Holy Spirit gives us. But the Father is good to us: when we ask for the Holy Spirit to come, He comes, and He brings with Him all the spiritual gifts He wants us to minister with at that moment.

2. Practice

Like all skills, we can grow in our ability to minister in the power of the Spirit. This involves practice, and lots of it. Each of us has something to share, a testimony, or an impartation of the Holy Spirit. We must practice sharing what we have, even if it seems too little or unimportant to make a difference.

Consider Jesus' parable of the talents in Matthew 25. The servants who invested the talents entrusted to them were rewarded with more, while the one who kept it to himself out of fear was scolded, and what he did have was taken from him. Likewise, because the Holy Spirit resides in all believers, we all have a measure of spiritual gifting, whether or not we are aware of this fact or not. If we use what we have been given, we will be given more. If we don't, what we have will be taken from us. The gifts are not for us to keep; they are gifts for those around us. We must practice what we have been given in order to grow in the gifts.

You will likely make many mistakes, but there is comfort in knowing that you are doing ministry *with* the Holy Spirit. He is just as interested in what is happening in *you* as you partner with Him in ministry, as He is in what He is doing in the person you are ministering to.

Practice involves risk. It can feel precarious to step out and pray for the sick the first time. It can feel awkward to give a prophetic word to someone—even if you have done it a hundred times. Regardless, it is important to lay your fears aside and start practicing. You must start somewhere, even if it means starting small.

When I (Brian) was first exposed to the concept of the kingdom of God, I had to see it in Scripture and get a theological grasp on it. Once I had the biblical foundation, I wanted to see it put in action. I wanted to be around people who were advancing the kingdom through power ministry. I had never seen anyone do it in a naturally supernatural way before I met Charles. I had seen it on TV, and all I knew was that I didn't fit the mold I saw there. I was yearning to see something I could emulate. Seeing Charles minister put a hunger and thirst in me: I thought if he could do it, maybe I could do it.

My wife, Jeanine, and I had been attending a class Charles was teaching on healing. We had practiced some in our class, but other than that we were really inexperienced when it came to praying for healing. After the course, my wife and I went to her parents' house for the weekend. Her parents wanted to go out for the evening, and we decided to stay at the house with a sick relative. I said to Jeanine, "This is our chance to see if this healing stuff really works." This was our first opportunity to pray for the sick outside of our little small group. Being the great man of faith that I was, I franticly locked all the doors and closed all the blinds because I was absolutely frightened that her parents would come back home or a neighbor would see us while we were praying.

So there was the sick relative, sleeping on the couch. The only thing I had with me was a manual Charles had given me which included John Wimber's five-step healing model. Upon receiving that manual, I was certain I had found the secret of the universe! We walked up to the sick relative and opened our manual. There is one part in the five step model that is really great, but sometimes it's hard to do. Here was my issue: step one of the healing model is the interview, and we had a huge communication barrier. The sick relative didn't speak English. In fact, the sick relative didn't speak any known language, because this beloved family relative was a dog. Snuggles the poodle didn't speak human, and I didn't speak dog, so the interview was pretty much out of the question.

I knew that Snuggles had a stomach condition; he could only crawl along on his belly because he was too uncomfortable to walk. I didn't know much else. I couldn't ask, "Did you eat some bad Kibbles and Bits?" or "Are you demonized?"

I did everything you could think of for that dog. I prayed every prayer I could imagine. I cast out every devil I could think of, but since I couldn't interview Snuggles, I didn't know if anything was happening. How was I going to be able to see the effects of my prayer?

I took poor Snuggles and I prayed, "Oh God, I sure hope this works." I lifted Snuggles up over my head and prayed one last hopeful prayer: "Lord Jesus, please let your healing come!"... and I let go of Snuggles, dropping him to the ground.

Poor Snuggles died that day. Not really! Actually, Snuggles ran off completely healed. I was completely shocked. I thought, *No way! How did that possibly work?* I was amazed.

That was how I started praying for the sick. I love that Jesus says the way to start is to be faithful in small things. I started by being faithful with a dog. Because I took the risk to be faithful with a dog, now, thirteen years later, I can honestly say I have seen the lame walk, the blind see, and the deaf hear. I have seen countless healings—not because I'm a great anointed man of God, but because I have stumbled along with many years of practicing. My only success has been by the grace of God.

3. Prepare

It is important that we take time to prepare. We should spend time studying spiritual gifts and effective Spirit-empowered ministry. The biggest resource we have is Scripture. Read Scripture with the viewpoint that God is unchanging; what He did in the Bible He still does today. What He did through His people *then* He desires to do through you *now*. With regard to growing in the power gifts, it is especially helpful to study the Gospels and Acts with the eyes of a disciple wanting to emulate what you see Jesus and His early disciples doing.

There are also many other resources available to help you grow in spiritual gifts. Any Christian bookstore will likely have a large variety of books to choose from on the topic. Read biographies of champions of the faith. Read theological books that will stretch your intellect as well as your faith. You can also find many video and audio resources online. Commit yourself to being a learner, and then put what you learn into practice. In the back of this book we have a list of resources which have helped us along the way.

4. Proximity

Spiritual gifts are not for us; they are for those people whom God loves that we are ministering to. Therefore, we must be around people to use spiritual gifts. If we hide ourselves from the world, God cannot use us to minister to the world. If you want to grow in healing, get around sick people. The gift of healing will only be expressed around sick people. If you want to grow in evangelism, get around lost people. If you want to grow in prophecy, get around discouraged people. Put yourself in positions where the gift of God in you is needed.

5. People

Jesus' disciples learned by watching Jesus and doing ministry with Jesus. We learn best the same way. Get around people who are already walking in power ministry. Talk with them, learn from them, go where they go, and do the things they do. If there is someone whose faith challenges you, stick with them and emulate them until what they have becomes yours as well.

We see an example of this in 1 Samuel 10:1-8 when Samuel instructed Saul to meet up with a group of prophets. "The Spirit of the LORD will come powerfully upon you, and you will prophesy with them; and you will be changed into a different person." Likewise, we are changed as we surround ourselves with people who can teach us and impart something to us. We see the same thing in the New Testament with Paul when he encouraged the believers in Corinth to follow his example as he followed Christ (1 Corinthians 11:1). We learn from Christ as we submit ourselves to learn from others who are more proficient in the power ministry gifts than we are.

A corollary to this concept is that you have something to give as well. No matter how small, you have been given some measure of gifting and relationship with the Holy Spirit. Share what you have with other followers of Jesus who are less experienced than you. As you share what you have with others, God will bless you with more.

A few years ago, I (Brian) got the opportunity to tag along and do ministry with a friend of mine named Don Pirozok. He's a really gifted prophetic minister, and I was excited to get around him and learn from him. He had come from out of state to minister at our church, after which he would be traveling around to a few other churches in our area. Don has a strong prophetic gifting, but he had really been pressing in to see a lot of healing and miracles. I was riding with him on the way to a meeting at another church. Don was telling me about all these incredible things he had been seeing. He talked about legs growing out.

To be honest, I was a little put off when he began to talk about that. I thought it could be seen as a parlor trick. Offense rose up in my heart and I was full of cynicism. I had a hard time believing it, and I told Don. I was upfront with him about my doubts about it—not in a harsh way, in an honest way.

Don opened the meeting that night by asking how many people know that they have one leg shorter than the other. To my amazement, several hands lifted acknowledging that this was their condition. He narrowed it down, asking for only the people who had a greater than one inch difference. With several people raising their hands, Don said, "Great! My friend Brian here has great faith to see legs grow out." I thought to myself, *You jerk! What are you doing?!*

Don had the people come forward, and I put my game face on while thinking, *How quickly can I get through this?* These people think I have this great faith and gifting for legs to grow. If they only knew the real conversation Don and I had had, they wouldn't have wanted me to pray for them. I had been thrown into a game I didn't want to play. We had people sit straight up in a chair with their hips square and all the way back. We had them straighten their legs out so we could see the differences in length between the two legs. To my amazement there really were major differences—one to three inch differences in some people.

I decided the best strategy was to pray a quick, short prayer to get it over with, then push the other prayer team members up, and I'd move on really quickly before anyone realized that I didn't actually believe in this stuff.

Then I heard a lady screaming "Oh my gosh! It worked!"

I rolled my eyes. *Come on lady, you just want this to happen.* I still don't know why I had so much cynicism, but I did.

I went back to the lady because she was so hysterically excited. She showed me her legs. I had seen the difference in her legs before, and to my surprise they were normal. She was completely overjoyed, so it was hard to be cynical around someone so thrilled. I started to think maybe there was something to this thing.

What happened next definitely pushed me beyond what little faith I had just gained. She excitedly said, "It's amazing that you can grow out legs. Can you grow out other things, too?"

My imagination went every which way about what she could be asking. *What did she want me to grow out?* Did she realize that ten minutes ago I didn't believe any of this and that she was the first person I had ever seen healed of this condition?

I very cautiously said, "Sure, I guess. What do you want grown out?"

She took me over to a teenage girl and said, "Can you grow her toe out?" I looked down and saw that the tip of the girl's toe had been cut off maybe a quarter to a half inch. My friend Jon was already praying with her. The girl was the niece of his former boss, who was also there.

We interviewed the girl and found out she had cut off the tip of her toe in a lawn mower accident. She told us we could pray for her toe, but we couldn't touch it because of the intense pain. She said, "It is so sensitive that I will scream and hit you if you touch my toe!"

I thought, *what have I gotten myself into?* Moments before I didn't even believe legs could grow, then I saw it happen. Now I wouldn't believe that toes could grow. Once again, I decided I was going to do one of those quick prayers and pass it on to Jon. I prayed and was turning to walk away when I heard the lady scream again, "Oh my gosh! It worked!"

I thought, *No way! You are just wanting to believe.* (What's so wrong with wanting to believe, anyway?) All I can say is that my mind definitely needed to be renewed that night.

I looked back and I didn't see anything different. I was expecting (if anything happened at all) the tip of the toe would form flesh and the nail would grow. It still looked like a chopped off toe to me. But the girl said, "No, I feel something. It's different." As I looked closer I saw that the length of the toe had grown out so that the cut-off tip reached to the height the toe should be.

Still not being a great man of faith, still being skeptical and full of doubt, I asked "Are you sure?" Then I remembered what she had told me before we prayed. *Don't even touch my toe. I will scream and hit you.* I said skeptically, "You believe something really happened, huh?"

"Yeah, don't you believe this stuff?" She looked at me like I was stupid.

"Do you trust me?," I asked.

"Yes, I trust you."

Remembering how intensely she described the pain, I asked one more time, "Are you sure?" She was.

I'm not advocating what I did, but I had to find out if it was true or not. I grabbed her toe and flicked it with my finger as hard as I could, not once but three or four times. She stared at me—didn't scream, didn't hit. She said, "If I wouldn't have been healed, I would have punched you in the mouth and screamed at you."

A few months later, my friend Jon ran into his former boss again. They got to talking about that night, and she told Jon that her niece's toe nail and skin eventually grew back so that it looked like a normal toe.

My faith was challenged that night, and I grew in an experiential knowledge of God's ability to heal. As much as I was mad at Don at the beginning of the evening, I was thankful for what he had done. We need people in our lives who push us into realities that we wouldn't have experienced otherwise.

6. Place

Find environments which are conducive to experimenting with and growing in spiritual gifts. For example, find a group of friends who are on the same spiritual journey, and share your experiences with each other. Pray for each other and share accountability and encouragement with each other. Look for places where it is safe to practice spiritual gifts, such as home groups. In the safety of an environment of believers who challenge each other on to further growth and maturity, you can share impressions and prayers without fear of rejection or the embarrassment of being wrong. Begin to practice getting prophetic words for each other. Pray for healing over any condition, no matter how small. Do whatever you can in a safe learning environment to grow and develop your spiritual gifts so that you have the confidence to minister to people "in the streets."

7. Personality

God made you uniquely you because He likes you that way. Therefore, spiritual gifts in you are going to be expressed through your personality. You don't have to become someone you are not in order to operate in spiritual gifts or be used in power evangelism. God is shaping and molding you into the person He has uniquely created you to be. His gifts and calling will reflect His destiny and purpose for you.

The gifts God gives you have been tailor-made to work hand in hand with God in you. The Father is not looking for spiritual clones. Though we often become like the people we learn from and surround ourselves with, He desires to do something unique through you that will look like Him in you. Don't worry about having a different style or approach than others. Let them do it their way and give yourself permission to do it your way. There is great comfort and wonder in knowing that God is doing what God can only do through you.

8. Purity

To try to minister like Jesus while living like the devil is a contradiction of lifestyle no one can maintain. Ministry to others is obedience pointed outward; holiness and purity is obedience pointed inward. Obedience in both directions must be maintained if ministry is to be sustained. God empowers us as imperfect people while at the same time moving us toward Christlikeness in character. To cooperate with God in ministry while resisting Him in purity will always lead to disaster and hypocrisy. Success in ministry at the expense of personal integrity is no success at all.

Paul shares a long discourse on the operation and proper use of spiritual gifts in 1 Corinthians chapters 12 through 14. Sandwiched in between the two great chapters on spiritual gifts lies chapter 13, commonly called "the love chapter". Paul gently reminds us in this chapter that spiritual gifts are an expression of love, and without love ministry has no value at all. Without love, tongues just sound like clanging cymbals to both God and our hearers. Without love, our prophetic words mean nothing. Love is to be at the center of all we do.

The Holy Spirit distributes the gifts as He wills, and even the most immature of believers can operate in gifts because the gifts are available to all believers. However, love refines the use of the gifts so that we use them with the precision of a surgeon's scalpel rather than the abrupt brutality of a butcher's knife. When our motivations for ministry are purely rooted in love for God and love for others, our effectiveness increases.

People can sense when we are praying for them with religious compunction or when we are trying to bring glory to ourselves. We are constantly going through sanctification, so our motives will involve a mix of the pure and impure. Our aim should be to identify the impure motivations and humbly submit them to the Lord. It is when we are motivated by a pure heart desiring to serve people and bring glory to Jesus that the Holy Spirit is most able to move through us.

9. Persecution

Here in the United States we have little threat to our physical lives for living out the gospel; however, we should expect there to be pushback for living a gospel-centered life. We are in a spiritual war in which the powers of darkness are doing everything they can to prevent us from advancing the kingdom of God. We should expect resistance. We should expect to be misunderstood and challenged, even from the people closest to us. Jesus was often misunderstood; even the disciples didn't fully understand what Jesus had been teaching them about His death until after the resurrection. Likewise, there will be people who just don't "get you" and may even oppose you.

We cannot misinterpret opposition as God's way of saying we are on the wrong path. If we keep our convictions about the love of God for the people around us (and for us) central in our focus, we will be less-easily swayed by persecution. Our hope and security lies in Christ, not in how the world around us responds to our obedience.

10. Perseverance

Learning to see, hear, and do the works of the Father does not come easily to most people. Learning any new skill requires patience and persistence. John Wimber used to say you can stop praying for the sick after you have tried one hundred times and failed every time. Praying effectively for others is like learning to ride a bicycle without wobbling or learning to swim without sinking—these are acquired skills that require perseverance.

There have been many occasions when we have both been disappointed and dissatisfied at our lack of effectiveness. More than once we have been tempted to throw in the towel and quit; but we always return to our conviction that empowered ministry is something Jesus passed on to the church, and the Holy Spirit has been given to us to continue this work. Compassion for others and the conviction of our commission fuel our perseverance.

11. Personal Relationship

All true ministry is ministry with the Father. It is out of relationship with Him that compassion for others and a sense of calling is cultivated. As we are rooted and grounded in His love for us, we hear Him beckoning us to come closer to Him and closer to those He loves, living in both the sanctuary and the street.

A striking transformation takes place in us as we partner with the Father in doing His ministry on the earth. We minister to others, but in the process He is also transforming us, molding us more and more into the image of Christ. As we recognize His work both in us and through us, we recognize the transformational depths of His love for us and the depths of His love for others.

Jeanine Blount, Brian's wife, shares a powerful example of how God works in us while He also reaches out to the world through us.

One Sunday at church, during Charles' sermon, I felt God strongly tugging at my heart and calling me back to a lifestyle of evangelism. At the time, we had our first of six children. She was nine months old, and I was totally overwhelmed with being a new mom. On top of this, we had recently taken in a teenage foster daughter who was grieving over the recent death of her mother. I felt like my home life was on overload. When God started speaking to me about evangelism, my honest reaction was anger. *How can I evangelize if I never leave my house!? I'm stuck there all day long with the baby!* I was ticked off that God was giving me what seemed like an impossible assignment. So this was my angry, honest, sarcastic prayer that day: "God, if you want me to evangelize, then you will have to bring them to my door!" I don't think I would have prayed that prayer if I had known how literally God wanted to answer it.

Several days later, my daughter was having a particularly fussy day. I had tried all the usual things to calm her, but all she would do was cry. It was one of the first nice afternoons of springtime, so I thought maybe she would like sitting outside on the front lawn. As soon as I did, she calmed down, so I decided to spend as long as it took there on the grass in front of our house. After a while, I heard frantic knocking on my neighbor's door. I looked over and saw a naked lady with a look of sheer terror on her face. That's right. Naked! 100 percent naked.

I spoke up and said, "Can I help you?"

As soon as she turned and saw me, she ran toward my house, past me, through the front door, and into my living room where she was trying to hide in a corner saying, "I'm naked! I'm naked!"

I gave her a nearby blanket then headed to my room to find her some clothes. While she was changing, I went to Brian's office. He had been working during this time and had no idea what had transpired. I told him about the lady, and once she had calmed down, she was able to share her story with us. She had been visiting a boyfriend who lived about ten houses down the street. Long story short, she became afraid for her life and escaped out of a small bathroom window. From there she began knocking on every door, trying to get help before the boyfriend realized she had escaped. To this day, I am amazed at how God protected and covered this woman past every house on our street so that I was the only person who ever saw her naked, and that no further harm came to her from knocking on the wrong person's door.

Brian and I were able to tell her that it was no accident she ran into our house. God knew that she was desperate for help, and He knew that what she really needed was Him. We were able to share the gospel with her and pray with her. She was absolutely overwhelmed not just with her situation, but with everything God was saying to her at that very moment. It was a sovereign moment in which the hand of the Lord was mightily on her.

I will never forget that day or the prayer I'd prayed the Sunday before. God wanted to get two people's attention that afternoon, both that lady's and mine. I learned something new that day: God is much more ready to break into my life and use me than I think. My current life situation, no matter how busy or stuck I think I am, doesn't dissuade Him from His love for me or His desire for me to partner with Him to love on His children. Every excuse we have is just that—an excuse. A lesson I learned from a naked lady.

12. Processing

Ministry can be a catalyst for transformation. We must be careful not to let the busyness of ministry or life distract us from paying attention to the interior work of God in our own souls.

Ministry to others offers the opportunity of personal transformation, but for many it is an opportunity ignored. We must find the time to process what God is doing in us while He is ministering through us. There always remains the danger and temptation of slipping into a ministry-driven relationship with God at the expense of an intimacy-driven relationship. A great prayer model for learning to process life in God's presence is the Examen discussed in chapter five.

Prayer Models

There are no magic formulas in the kingdom of God. There are no magic words we can say that will make healing come or cause someone to experience the presence of God. However, it is helpful to have some sort of road map which gives us something to go on when we don't feel like we have specific direction from the Holy Spirit. Prayer models don't cause ministry to happen; they simply provide a tool to assist in hearing and seeing what the Father is doing. They give us a starting point for receiving direction in how to pray for people.

One of the most assessable models we practice is the five step prayer model popularized by John Wimber while he was teaching at Fuller Seminary in the 1980s. This model can be modified to fit most ministry opportunities. We will give a very brief synopsis of it here.[7]

1. **Interview**. Ask the person what is wrong with him. This need not be lengthy, but just enough to get the basic idea of what the symptoms are. Simultaneously, be listening to the person and listening to God for His insight on what is happening in his body.
2. **Diagnostic Decision**. Determine the root source of the condition. Is the source physical, such as a virus or an injury?

Is it emotionally or spiritually related, such as health problems stemming from stress, anxiety, or unforgiveness? Is it demonic in nature, meaning the condition is being caused by demonic oppression afflicting the person? Many people assume only a physical cause to their conditions, but this is most often not the case. The root cause may even be a combination of all the above.

3. **Prayer Selection.** Our diagnostic decision will determine our prayer selection. If we feel that the source is demonic, we pray deliverance prayers. If we feel the source is emotional or spiritual, we pray for spiritual or emotional healing to come to these areas of the person's life. If it is physical, we pray healing over the physical conditions.

4. **Prayer Engagement.** This is where we actually start praying. During the course of the prayer time, we are continually asking the person what he is experiencing and if he is receiving any healing or other effects from our prayers. We continue to ask the Father to give us insight as well. Sometimes the Father reveals something new while we are praying and we go back through the first four steps again. We continue to pray for the person until he is healed or there is a sense that the prayer time is concluded.

5. **Post-Prayer Directions.** Offer helpful instructions the person might need to continue to receive healing in his life. If you prayed for emotional or spiritual issues or for deliverance, the person may feel very vulnerable. Assure him of your love and God's love for him, and help him connect with other people who can support him in the healing work God is doing in his life.

We have used this model for years as a springboard to help us pray for others. There may be times when the Holy Spirit gives specific instructions and none of these steps are needed, but those instances are the exception. Most often, we begin with the prayer model and allow the Holy Spirit to lead us from there. Many times we stick to the model throughout the time we are praying for the person, and other less frequent times we start with it and then sense the Holy Spirit move us in another direction altogether. In every case, our reliance should always be on the Holy Spirit and His ability to minister to the person, not on the model we are using.

Over the course of many years practicing power evangelism, I (Brian) have found the need to modify Wimber's model slightly to fit the needs of the awkwardness that accompanies ministry to strangers "in the streets." Wimber's model is great for many settings, but it does little to help with knowing how to do a "cold approach" with someone you have never met and gain his trust enough for him to allow you to pray for him. Also, on the streets, it is often necessary to do the entire exchange in a short amount of time, such as when you are in a check-out line at a store. Over time—through lots of trial and error and mistakes—I have found out what works well for me. This is the basic model that I tend to follow when I am praying for people on the streets.

1. **Approach.** Approaching a stranger to ask if you can pray for them is sometimes the most awkward part of the process. First, introduce yourself briefly with just your name. You can put the person on the defensive if you start off by saying you go to such-and-such church or you want to pray for him. You can ask him his name if he doesn't offer it. What you say after the introductions depends on whether or not you feel like the Holy Spirit has given you revelation about the person.

   When You Feel Like God Has Given You an Impression
   If you have received some sort of prophetic impression for them, share it in a very non-religious way such as

"Sometimes I sense things about people, and this was the sense I had when I saw you..." If you feel like you have a word of knowledge for healing say something like, "I know this may sound weird, but do you happen to have a problem with..." Approach the situation with humility. Your impressions may be incorrect or partial, so use phrases like "I think..." or "I get the sense..."

When You Can Tell They Need Healing

Sometimes you may approach someone because you can see that there is something physically wrong with him. Maybe he walks with a limp or he has medical equipment with him. You could start by saying, "Hey, I noticed the sling on your arm. Do you mind telling me what happened to you?" People are often very willing to talk about their physical conditions. If they are not, don't push them. They may not be open to you praying for them, and that's okay too.

Other Ways to Approach People

Through the years, I have tried many other methods to approach people. Depending on your personality and the people you are attempting to engage, you might try one of these approaches. They may be helpful to you as is, or they may prompt other ideas that would work better for you. Again, no approach will likely feel comfortable at first, so just try out a few and see what works for you.

- "Excuse me, but I was wondering if there might be any need in your life that I might pray for." After what is often a shocked or quizzical look, you follow up with, "I know this might sound strange, but I simply like to pray for people. Is there anything I might pray for you?"
- "I have some good news for you. Jesus said that His presence is near, not far away. That might seem crazy, but it's true. May I prove it's true by praying for you?"

- "Hey, could I demonstrate the love of God to you in a practical way by praying for you?"
- "I was wondering if you could help me with something. I've been learning some new things, and I have an experiment I'm working on. I'm learning how to hear God for others (or pray for the sick), and I was wondering if you wouldn't mind being my guinea pig and letting me practice with you."
- "Are you familiar with the Lord's Prayer? Remember the part about 'your will be done on earth as it is in heaven'? These aren't just poetic words, but Jesus meant for us to demonstrate the reality of heaven on earth. May I pray for you?"

2. **Interview.** This step is much like Wimber's interview step, but it's easier for me to put Wimber's diagnostic decision and prayer selection in here with the interview. While we talk with the person, we are doing spiritual multi-tasking. We listen to the person talk about his physical condition or the prophetic word or impression we shared. We also listen to the Holy Spirit as He tells us His perspective on the situation. At the same time, we are trying to discern the sources of influence in the situation: is this situation emotional, spiritual, demonic, or physical in nature?

   If he is in need of healing, ask specific questions that will help you know how effective your prayers are. For example, you can ask him how bad the symptoms are right then on a scale from one to ten. This will help out later during the prayer time so you can know if healing is happening or not. Another good question to ask is how long the condition has been going on. Many times, emotionally and spiritually rooted symptoms begin at the time of some emotional hurt or spiritual need. If the pain began three years previously, ask the person if there was anything significant that was happening in his life three years before.

If you are sharing a prophetic word of encouragement for someone, you may not even need to go on to the next step of prayer. Sharing the impression you received may be all you need to do at the time. Just let the person know that the only reason you would know anything about him is because Jesus loves him and He wanted to express His love for him in a way that was meaningful to him.

Remember to keep the entire conversation non-religious. Avoid religious language. Talk to him in the way two people normally talk when they strike up a conversation to get to know each another.

3. **Prayer.** It is always awkward knowing how to begin praying for the person. Up to this point, he may have no idea that you are a Christian who believes in healing who desires to pray for him. You can begin by saying something like, "I believe in the power of prayer. Do you mind if I pray for you?" You do not need to lay hands on the person when you pray for him, unless you feel the Holy Spirit impressing you to do so. If you do lay hands on him, ask his permission first and do it in a considerate way. If you have the gift of tongues, or what some people call a prayer language, you might want to avoid using this or anything else that might cause him to feel uncomfortable as you pray.

As you pray, invite the Holy Spirit to come and touch the person. Pray short, to the point prayers; after all, it is the Holy Spirit who brings the ministry, not our many words. Depending on the setting, you may have only a few precious seconds to pray. It's helpful to keep your eyes open as you pray so that you can see what is happening with the person.

Sometimes you may see a manifestation of the Holy Spirit's presence come on the person as you watch him, such as deepened breathing, trembling, swaying, or crying. You may also experience similar phenomena in your body, too, as an indication of the presence of God. Don't be surprised by God's desire to show up in a tangible, physical way.

4. **Assessment.** As you pray, ask the person if he is feeling anything. People will often sense the Lord's presence, though they may not have language for what they are experiencing. They may feel immediate or partial relief from their condition if they were in need of healing. Ask the person what is happening in his body. If you are praying for healing, ask him to move the afflicted part of his body to see if there is any change.

Continue to listen to the Holy Spirit for further direction about how to pray, and go back into prayer as you feel led. Unless the person receives complete healing of his condition, there is no clear cut way to know when to stop praying. You must be tuned into several factors. Has the Holy Spirit apparently finished doing what He was doing in this situation? Is the person indicating prayer should stop by his words or body language? Have you run out of insight on what to do next? Be sensitive to the person you are praying for. Remember that he should always leave the situation feeling loved by you and loved by God.

More often than not, if you are able to get to the point of praying for someone, something significant will happen. He will receive healing or he will sense the Lord's presence in some way. He will often want to talk about what he experienced. Tell him that this happened because Jesus loves him and wants to make Himself known to him. Share the gospel with him in a non-religious manner, and encourage him that he can trust Jesus because He knows him and loves him.

Although models like this are helpful, no model can alter the fact that praying for people "in the streets" is often uncomfortable, awkward, and sometimes embarrassing. The reason we pray for people, however, is not just because it is rewarding, although sometimes it is. We pray for people because we seek to bring glory to Jesus and we are convinced that it is His desire to reach the world today through ordinary people like us.

Insight Seven: Faith Is Spelled R-I-S-K

Our challenge is to take risks for the sake of the kingdom.

Ministry always involves taking a risk. Risk always involves wrestling with doubt and the danger of appearing foolish. It is risky to approach a stranger and share an impression we have for him. It is risky to pray for the sick, whether it's praying healing for a mild headache or for blindness. We risk being wrong. We risk looking like idiots. We risk being chastised or challenged for our beliefs. However, there is also the possibility that if we take the risk someone could come away changed forever by the power of Jesus Christ.

Through the years, we have gained a lot of experience in praying for the sick and doing power evangelism on the streets. One thing we have learned is that it never gets easy. It never stops feeling awkward. We never stop questioning whether the impressions we think we get are correct or not. We never stop having butterflies in our stomachs. We never stop wondering if we are going to be rejected. Sometimes the fears are easy to push aside, and sometimes they are not. We have learned to put our game faces on while, on the inside, we are screaming, *"O God, o God! Help!"* We may have become better at pressing past these thoughts and fears, but they are always present, lingering in the recesses of our minds.

Foolishness

Concerning the issue of appearing foolish, the Bible has much to say. To begin with, God is not primarily concerned about how we appear to others. He allowed His own Son to appear foolish to the world when He died on the cross. In fact, it seems that appearing foolish is one of the means God uses to promote His purposes in the world.

> *For the message of the cross is foolishness to those who are perishing, but to us who are being saved it is the power of God. For it is written: "I will destroy the wisdom of the wise; the intelligence of the intelligent I will frustrate." Where is the wise man? Where is the scholar? Where is the philosopher of this age? Has not God made foolish the wisdom of the world?*

> *For since in the wisdom of God the world through its wisdom did not know him, God was pleased through the foolishness of what was preached to save those who believe. Jews demand miraculous signs and Greeks look for wisdom, but we preach Christ crucified: a stumbling block to Jews and foolishness to Gentiles, but to those whom God has called, both Jews and Greeks, Christ the power of God and the wisdom of God. For the foolishness of God is wiser than man's wisdom, and the weakness of God is stronger than man's strength.*

> *Brothers, think of what you were when you were called. Not many of you were wise by human standards; not many were influential; not many were of noble birth. But God chose the foolish things of the world to shame the wise; God chose the weak things of the world to shame the strong. He chose the lowly things of this world and the despised things—and the things that are not—to nullify the things that are, so that no one may boast before him. (1 Corinthians 1:18-29)*

Paul continues with this thought when describing the ministry he and his fellow apostles had been given.

For it seems to me that God has put us apostles on display at the end of the procession, like men condemned to die in the arena. We have been made a spectacle to the whole universe, to angels as well as to men. We are fools for Christ, but you are so wise in Christ! We are weak, but you are strong! You are honored, we are dishonored! To this very hour we go hungry and thirsty, we are in rags, we are brutally treated, we are homeless. We work hard with our own hands. When we are cursed, we bless; when we are persecuted, we endure it; when we are slandered, we answer kindly. Up to this moment we have become the scum of the earth, the refuse of the world. (1 Corinthians 4:9-13)

The willingness to appear foolish in the eyes of the world, and at times even in the eyes of the church, is often a prerequisite for moving in the power of God. As much as we might wish there was another way, there is not. Appearing cool and detached has become a value in our culture. Taking risks, on the other hand, is counter to our culture. But there is no other way. In the parable of the talents (Matthew 25:24-30), it was the servant who refused to take a risk that was called "wicked and lazy."

For many of us, if we could be assured of success, then the trauma of taking a risk would be greatly reduced, but it does not work this way. Jesus does not guarantee success for every endeavor we take or every attempt to respond to Him in obedience. When Jesus sent out the seventy-two nameless disciples to preach the gospel, He did not guarantee them success; in fact, He warned them of the very opposite. "But when you enter a town and are not welcomed...be sure of this: The kingdom of God is near" (Luke 10:10-11). What we find so encouraging in these words is that the kingdom of God is near even when we fail or fall short.

Brennan Manning, in his book *Ruthless Trust,* recounts this story:

> *When the brilliant ethicist John Kavanaugh went to work for three months at "the house of the dying" in Calcutta, he was seeking a clear answer as to how best to spend the rest of his life. On the first morning there he met Mother Teresa. She asked, "What can I do for you?" Kavanaugh asked her to pray for him.*
>
> *"What do you want me to pray for?" she asked. He voiced the request that he had borne thousands of miles from the United States: "Pray that I have clarity."*
>
> *She said firmly, "No, I will not do that." When he asked her why, she said, "Clarity is the last thing you are clinging to and must let go of." When Kavanaugh commented that she always seemed to have the clarity he longed for, she laughed and said, "I have never had clarity; what I have always had is trust. So I will pray that you trust God."[8]*

Manning goes on to articulate that craving clarity is an attempt to eliminate the risk of trusting in the goodness and love of God. The inspiration for *Ruthless Trust* came from a challenge from his spiritual director who told him, "Brennan, you don't need any more insights into the faith. You've got enough insights to last you three hundred years. The most urgent need in your life is to trust what you have received."[9] For many of us, the challenge is the same.

We must believe that what we have received from God is really from Him. Our faith does not rest in the fact that we have great ability to discern Him. It rests in His goodness, His love for others, and His desire to reach them through us. Yes, we get our wires crossed from time to time; yes, we miss it more often than we would like; and yes, our prayers for healing are not always answered. But we take great risks because of God's great love. John Wimber used to tell us that faith is spelled R-I-S-K. We would add that love is spelled exactly the same way.

It always feels safer to teach about healing than to actually step out in faith to pray for the sick. In some portions of the church, people are taught to have faith for healing, and then if they're not healed through prayer, they are blamed for not having enough faith. By contrast, the people Jesus rebuked for not having enough faith for healing were His disciples—the ones called and commissioned by Him to heal the sick. We who are followers of Jesus are called to take risks for the sake of the kingdom.

Risk-taking means that we consider the potential for healing and relief from suffering a higher value than looking good and respectable. Failure is the price we sometimes pay for the opportunity to be successful from time to time. If we don't pray for the sick, no one gets healed through prayer, but when we do pray, some are healed. It is Christ's love that compels us to pray.

Risking it for the Deaf

During a mission trip to Romania, we were holding services in the evenings at a church. We had spent the afternoon sending teams of people out to the villages to pray for the sick and had invited people to attend the service that night. One of the villagers who came was a man who was completely deaf in one ear. I (Brian) asked him if he would come forward so we could pray for him. He agreed, and I began praying for hearing to come back into his ear. I felt so much compassion for this man and I desperately wanted him to be able to hear again. I kept praying and praying. I would stop every once in a while to interview him, but every time he said there was no difference. I continued to pray. I was persistent—I really wanted to see this man healed. I hated his deafness, and compassion for this man drove me to continue praying. I was determined to see his deafness leave.

As time passed, I could tell the other people in the room were starting to get uncomfortable. Some of the members of our ministry team were beginning to feel awkward as I continued to pray to no avail. A nervous laughter began to reverberate around the room as the tension mounted. It's a little disconcerting to watch someone else try and try for healing with no result, especially in such a public setting.

The nervous laughter didn't concern me. In fact, it made me even more determined. I looked up and said to everyone, "Laugh if you want, but one day I will see the deaf healed!" I wasn't being arrogant; rather I was carrying a deep conviction that Jesus loves deaf people and wants to destroy deafness. The conviction in my voice silenced all laughter.

I eventually stopped praying for the man because we needed to move on with the service, but several other team members took the man outside to continue praying for him. He was not healed that night, but he was so touched by our prayers and our determination to help him that he gave his life to Jesus. He was saved because we were willing to risk looking foolish for his sake.

When we love people, we risk for them. I was stirred with the love of Jesus for this precious Romanian man, and as a result I hated everything that oppressed him. Because of that, I risked for him. I looked like a complete fool. Even my closest friends were laughing at me and giving up on me. So did I fail that night? I certainly think not. The man didn't receive his hearing. However, he was saved, and it stirred an even greater desire in me to see the deaf healed. I have taken the risk to pray for many deaf people since then, and many times I experienced the same frustration I did in Romania because nothing seemed to happen. Now I can honestly say that since my declaration of faith that night in Romania, I have seen about a dozen people healed of partial or complete deafness, mostly here in the United States.

Just Another Sunday Afternoon

Every Sunday after church my (Brian's) family has a pretty predictable pattern. Sundays are supposed to be restful, and the last thing my wife wants to do after church is cook lunch, so we always stop by McDonald's for the kids and then head to Arby's for Jeanine. Then we all head home with our take-out sacks and sit around the dining room table passing ketchup packets and soft drinks.

On this particular Sunday, we had experienced an awesome service at church. God had healed a lady in a remarkable way, so I was still on a bit of a high and excited to see God do more. We drove up to the drive-thru at McDonald's, and I felt like I had an impression for the cashier about him having a gifting for writing music. I shared the impression with him, and he quickly informed me that I was definitely wrong. Feeling slightly dejected, we left and headed to Arby's.

When I came to the Arby's window, I sensed the lady at the window had problems with headaches and neck pain. She had a very shy demeanor. We were waiting for our food so I said,

"Excuse me, this may be a strange question, but are you having a headache and neck pain right now?"

Timidly, she said her neck bothered her a lot, although it wasn't at the moment, and that her head was hurting her at that moment. She was bewildered and said "How did you know?"

I told her the only way I knew was because Jesus loves her and He knew about her life and pain. I asked if she would hold out her hand. I gently took it and said, "Jesus come and heal the headache and the neck pain. Amen."

She quietly said thank you and we took our food and drove away. She was so shy in her demeanor that there was no way to tell if she was experiencing anything or if she thought I was a total nut. After that, I really didn't think any more of it.

The next Sunday, we followed our same fast food routine. Once again, we came to the window at Arby's and I handed over my money to the attendant without even noticing it was the same girl. She just quietly smiled up at me and said, "Hi." Then I remembered what had happened the week before.

I asked, "So did you experience any relief from your headaches and neck pain?" She said yes, that she hadn't had any problems at all in the last week. She just kept looking at us and quietly smiling, like she wanted to say more but she was too shy to do so. I asked her what had happened when I prayed for her. She said that she had felt the pain gradually go away as I prayed for her until it was totally gone and it had never come back since. I told her that Jesus healed her because He is good and this was an example of how He loves her. Still she lingered, clearly touched by what had happened the week before. In fact, she had totally forgotten that she was supposed to be taking orders in the drive-thru, and one of her co-workers came up and took the headset off her head with annoyance while she stayed at the window with us. I told her that God loved her and He wanted to bless her. I thanked her for sharing what she had experienced, then we took our food and drove home.

I was so thankful that I had taken a risk with this sweet girl the week before, even though I had just failed a few minutes earlier at McDonald's. It always seems foolish when we step out of our comfort zone and share Jesus with strangers. It may even at times seem fruitless and not worth the risk. We have to stop thinking *What if God doesn't show up?* and instead change our thinking to *What if God does show up? What if His power comes?* When we take a risk and God shows up, we get to step into the role of delivery boy or girl, letting God give His gifts of power and love, freedom for the oppressed, and healing for the broken-hearted.

Do-Rag Healing

I have a favorite place I like to go to pray for people. It's an area in Oklahoma City off of Exchange Avenue. This region is known for high poverty and crime rates, so I'll often pray for people while I see drug deals happening and prostitutes soliciting customers nearby. It's a great place to practice power evangelism.

On one occasion I was with an evangelism team we had taken out to Exchange, and I noticed a young lady walking by. I said, "Hey, we're out sharing the love of God in really practical ways. Is there anything you need prayer for?"

She was a little taken aback at first, but also intrigued and excited. I had a couple of impressions for her which I shared about her, specifically, that she had a gift for writing and poetry. I told her that it was a gift from God to express her life and her emotions. She acknowledged this to be true but went on to talk about her mom. "You can pray for me if you like, but my mom is in prison. She has diabetes and a lot of other health problems. I just found out that she is in a diabetic coma, and she is dying."

She had a do-rag scarf on her head. I said, "Are you going to be visiting your mom anytime soon?" She said no. Then I asked, "Can I have the do-rag from your head?" She agreed. "I know this sounds crazy, but there's a story in the Bible about these guys who would pray over cloths and send them to people who were sick, and they would be healed. So we are going to pray over the do-rag, and then you can send it to your mom." Then these words came out of my mouth: "...and she will be healed."

Oh, how I wanted to take those words back! I wanted to pull them out of the air and stuff them back in my mouth. *What was I thinking! What if she wasn't healed?*

She said, "Okay, I will."

We talked to her a couple more minutes, and then we each went our own way, never expecting to see each other again.

Months later, I was out on Exchange again, doing power evangelism with a friend, when I saw her walking around talking on her phone. She saw me and told her friend on the phone she had to go while she hurried over to me.

"You'll never believe what happened! I sent the do-rag to my mom, and the day it arrived in the mail she came out of the coma!" She also thanked me for telling her about the poetry. She had won a lot of awards, and now her poetry was going all across the United States. "You didn't know any of that!" She was so excited that she took us over to her apartment and introduced us to her boyfriend and some other friends. She kept on saying, "This is the guy who prayed and my mom was healed!"

It takes risk every time we go out to Exchange Avenue. It took risk for me to pray over that girl's do-rag. I didn't have a word from God that we needed to pray over the do-rag. It just seemed like something to step out and try. I didn't mean to say that her mom would be healed, but the gift of faith which rose up in me from the Holy Spirit did. Because of the risks we took that day, a lady in prison is no longer in a coma, and her daughter received Christ's love for her and the destiny He has for her.

Taking a Risk in Ada, Oklahoma

All the stories we are sharing in this book involve risk, but when I think back to the time I felt the most foolish, Ada, Oklahoma is foremost in my mind.

My friend, Greg Roberson, lives in Ada. My friend, Ramey Redden, and I got in our car to head to Ada for the purpose of doing some power evangelism on the streets with Greg that day. On the way, Ramey received an impression that we would encounter someone with a right shoulder problem, so we were excited to see what would come of that. We met at Greg's house, and before we started out we decided to pray. Our prayer time felt very unanointed at first, but we began to worship and declare God's goodness. We asked God to empower us. We could feel the presence of the Lord in Greg's living room. As we prayed, a phrase kept coming to my mind over and over and over: "There's a shaking of awakening coming to Ada!"

I felt compelled to shout this phrase out to the neighborhood, even though I knew I would look like a complete idiot. So I stood out on Greg's front porch and shouted "There's a shaking of awakening coming to Ada!" What did I care if I looked foolish? I didn't live in Ada. I was wondering what the neighbors across the street were thinking. Did they think I was shouting directly at them? Even Greg piped up and said, "Dude, I have to live here!"

We went back to the living room and kept praying. At one point, I looked out the window and saw a car out on the street. A lady and a man were talking. A flood of impressions and words of knowledge came to me as I looked at them. I had seven very specific impressions about the lady. I knew things about her physical body—she suffered from anemia, among other things. To top it off, I heard the Lord say, "And by the way, she *loves* horses."

I was taken aback by these words, trying to process them. How would I go over and engage this lady in a conversation? I had a million questions and doubts rolling around in my mind. I needed to use the restroom, so I thought I'd take care of business, then tell the guys about the impressions I was getting so we could figure out how to make our approach.

After getting out of the restroom, the lady and the car were gone. I asked Greg if he had seen her, and I ran outside to see if they were farther down the road. No one appeared to be home across the street where I had just seen her. We prayed and asked God to give us another opportunity to speak with the lady.

We continued praying. Some of our prayer was really just nervous stalling. We were afraid to actually go out on the streets. It was much easier to just pray about going out on the streets. So we decided to pray for one another (more stalling). When we were praying over Greg, I had a vision of little kids in diapers running barefoot and playing in oil. It didn't make sense, but I shared it with Greg and Ramey anyway. It didn't mean anything to any of us, so I just put it aside.

After we prayed a little bit longer—even more stalling—I really wanted to start going door-to-door asking people if we could pray for them. I like to dive into the deep end, but Greg and Ramey wanted to start at the shallow end of the pool first by going to a coffee shop, a place that felt less threatening than the anonymous doors of the neighborhood. When we arrived at the coffee shop, we all ordered a drink and sat down. The shop was pretty empty; just the barista and one other couple were there. We were trying to figure out who to pray for and which of us would go first. We decided I would. I felt like I might have something for the barista.

I went up to her and said, "Hey, sometimes I get pictures and impressions for people. Do you mind if I share something with you?" She had one of those roll-your-eyes, "whatever" looks mixed with a sarcastic smile. I shared the impressions with her and asked if any of them made sense to her. She said no, not one of them. The shop was kind of small, so the other couple in the shop could overhear the conversation. I could hear the whispering of hecklers like resounding shouts in my ears. I said to the barista, "I'm not very good at this, am I?" She agreed with a laugh, and I thanked her for letting me share.

As we left the coffee shop, we really started questioning ourselves. *Did I get anything right? I'm such an idiot!* The wind was taken out of my sails. Instead of giving up, we decided to go to apartment complexes, where we went door-to-door asking if we could pray for people. I was sure we would see something happen. We spent about thirty to forty-five minutes knocking on doors, always keeping an eye out for the person with a bad right shoulder that Ramey had seen. We heard a slot of "no thank you" and "nobody's home." There were a couple of people who let us pray for them, but nothing happened as far as we could tell.

We tried one last door before we left. We knocked on the door and said we were out trying to be of service, loving on people, praying for people's needs. "Is anybody sick in your home? We just want to show you that Jesus' presence is near and close." Long story short, after talking to the guy, he told us that we needed to go back home and pray some more. It was a real faith killer. When the lost tell you that your prophetic ministry is bad, it feels like it's time to go home.

We decided to go back to Greg's house and call it a day. I was feeling beat up and defeated, like a dog with his tail tucked between his legs. We had such excitement and hunger to see this "shaking of awakening in Ada." What had happened? We gave each other the "at least we tried" pep talk.

As soon as we entered Greg's house, his wife, Carisa, began to apologize for the strong smell in the house. She had been resting when she noticed the time was 3:33, a time that speaks to her about God answering prayer (Jeremiah 33:3). She then noticed a strong smell of perfume and found her two daughters had accidentally broken an air freshener. The fragranced oil had spilled in the exact spot where I had been standing earlier shouting "There's a shaking of awakening coming to Ada." The girls had been laughing and playing around in their diapers in the oil. Greg, Ramey, and I all looked at each other stunned, eyes opened, mouths dropped. *No way!* That was the vision I had seen earlier! We told Carisa about the vision, and immediately we were filled with faith.

I looked out the front window and saw a group of guys right across the street, standing in the yard where I had seen the lady earlier. It was the same house that I had shouted at about the shaking of awakening coming to Ada. I said to the guys, "This is God! Let's go." Greg wasn't so enthusiastic. He said that the house belonged to a known drug dealer, but I was full of faith and knew that God was going to do something big.

We walked across the street, the three of us feeling emboldened, but still nervous to be walking into a large group of guys. I walked right up to a guy who was talking on his phone. "Hi! I'm Brian. I live in Oklahoma City. I'm here visiting your neighbor, my friend Greg."

He interrupted his phone call saying, "Hold on... now what do you want?"

I repeated myself. I went on to describe the lady I had seen earlier. He said she was his friend.

I asked, "Is she here?"

"No."

"Can you give her a call?"

"Why?"

Due to the vision I had received earlier and because of what happened with Carisa and the girls, I had a bold assurance and faith. So I said, "I have a message from God for her. Can you give her a call right now?"

He still had his phone to his ear, so he said into the phone, "Hey, I gotta go. This guy is saying something about having a message from God." He didn't seem too convinced, but he gave the girl a call anyway. "There's this guy over here saying he has a message from God for you," and then he handed the phone to me.

Speaking into the phone, I said to her, "I don't mean to freak you out, but earlier today you were over here at your friend's house. I saw you and all of a sudden I began to get these words from the Lord for you. I'm going to tell you the words, and will you please be honest with me and tell me whether they are true or not?" She agreed, so I began to list the seven impressions I had gotten earlier, and then I said, "And by the way, you *love* horses."

As I told her each thing, she began to say over and over again, "It's true! It's true!" as I heard her weeping on the other end of the phone. I asked if she could come to the house. She didn't think it was possible because she had to get her boyfriend to the bus station within an hour. I asked if she would stop by briefly on the way.

While we were waiting for the lady to arrive, Greg's drug dealing neighbor kept looking at me like the entire situation was way too weird for him. By this time, the other guys who were there had freaked out. We had tried to ask if they wanted prayer, but they wanted out of there quick, so they left. I asked Greg's neighbor if there was anything we could pray for while we waited. He said he had an eye condition and he could only see a few inches from his face.

We prayed for him briefly and asked him to test it out. He said he could see! We backed up five feet, then ten feet, then twenty feet, and finally half way down the block. He kept saying, "I can see! I can see!" We came back from the end of the block, and he was clearly freaked out. He began to tell us that the reason all the people had been at his house that day was because a friend of theirs had recently died of an overdose and they had attended the funeral together. He was saying, "This is so weird! We just had the funeral, and now you guys are talking about God, and I can see fine."

Around this time, Greg's brother came over because he had heard that we were in town, but he didn't know what had been happening. He said that as he pulled up to Greg's house, it literally felt like he had stepped into a different dimension. The atmosphere over the neighborhood had changed.

Soon, the lady I had spoken to on the phone pulled up. She got out of the car with her boyfriend, her baby, and her child. I introduced myself, and I shared the words again so that everyone could hear. Again, she said that all the words were true. We began to pray for her and minister the love of God to her.

As I was praying for her, Greg and Ramey were talking with the others. The boyfriend shared that he had a right shoulder problem. He was the person Ramey had received the word about earlier that day in the car. He said he could only move his arm to a certain point and it was very painful. He was heading out of town for work, and he didn't know if he would be able to do the work. As we prayed for him, he told us he began to feel heat and tingling. We asked him to do something he couldn't do before.

Now what happened next could only happen in Ada, Oklahoma. He reached over to his girlfriend and said, "Honey, give me the baby." He put the baby in his right hand and extended the baby over his head, exclaiming with his rural Oklahoma drawl, "I couldn't do that before!"

They had to leave right away because his bus was leaving town in just minutes, so we quickly prayed that Jesus would come near to them, and we told them Jesus loved them. They received everything we were saying and thanked us as they left. Everyone was amazed by what had happened, but there was one guy sitting on the porch who had been observing everything going on, who seemed a little stand offish.

Boldness came over me as I said "Hey you! Come over here." For whatever reason, he just got up and came over. We began to share the love of God with him, and we explained a little bit about what had been going on. We shared a few impressions we felt we had for him. We asked if we could pray for him. The guy was listening and engaged, but I could still feel that his guard was up. Greg said, "God really has a key for you. He's going to unlock your heart, and He's going to give you a key."

At that very moment, Greg looked down and saw something shiny down in the dirt. He poked around the ground and picked up an old treasure-looking key. He said, "It's a key kind of like this." My mouth dropped. Somehow, the Lord just manifested a key!

The guy freaked out and said, "What you are saying is all true! I can't believe you are showing me this key! I collect hundreds of keys just like this." He was totally undone; all his walls came down. We shared the love of God with him and led him in a prayer to give his life back to the Lord. We prayed for the power of God to come and touch him.

Afterward, we interviewed him to find out what he had experienced during our prayer. "All I can say is that it felt like I was being tasered when you guys prayed for me!" I wasn't sure I wanted to know how he knew what it felt like to be tasered, but it was awesome nonetheless.

The day had started out with lots of hope, followed by the crushing feeling of failure, and ended in people's lives being changed. We risked a lot that day. I risked looking foolish when I yelled out to the street. I risked being wrong with the lady at the coffee shop. We risked getting doors slammed in our faces at the apartments. And we risked our pride and more when we approached Greg's neighbor. But in the end, the kingdom of God came, and there was a shaking of awakening in Ada.

Insight Eight: The Importance of Routinization

Our challenge is to establish a sustainable Christ-centered routine which includes evangelism.

As we read through the Gospels, we see Jesus did ministry day-to-day as He went about His business. He ministered to the woman at the well while waiting on His disciples to get back with lunch. Jesus raised a young boy from the dead as He happened on a funeral procession when He entered a town (Luke 7:11-16). But there are also special times when He intentionally set out to do ministry in a new location. We see both spontaneity and intentionality in the ministry of Jesus.

For some of us, evangelism is as natural as water is to a duck. The joy and excitement of purposefully reaching out to others gives us life, and then having them respond positively feeds our soul at a very deep and profound level. For others, our experience of reaching out to those we don't know is more in line with Paul's instruction to Timothy: "endure hardship, do the work of an evangelist" (2 Timothy 4:5). We can think of a dozen activities and jobs we would rather do than evangelize.

Life is filled with activities and responsibilities we enjoy doing along with things we don't enjoy as much, even though we enjoy the rewards they give us. We may not enjoy exercising at the gym, but we do enjoy being able to bend over to tie our shoelaces. For some of us, evangelism does not come naturally. However, this activity, if done with humility and dependence on the Holy Spirit, brings with it the joy of participating in the great missional activity of God. There is perhaps no greater joy to be had than finishing the day knowing that God used your obedience to advance the kingdom.

The monastic community has a phrase: "Rule of life." Rule of life is a personal and corporate regular rhythm which enables a follower of Christ to establish a pattern for living a balanced life. The understanding behind this is that life is too important to be left to chance. For people living in monasteries, this usually involves prayer, study of the Scriptures, and manual labor.

We all need a rule of life to keep us moving forward. The modern application of a rule of life is routinization. Routinization is the establishment of a pattern or routine. Many of us have established routines which include going to work, engaging in family activities, eating dinner, and worshiping with a faith community. Routines are sometimes seen as hindering creativity and life, but all successful musicians, athletes, and writers have one thing in common: they practice their craft over and over again. They dedicate time for practice by creating structure in their daily lives; they create routine. It is important to establish a routine that includes personal evangelism.

While we should always be ready for spontaneous opportunities which present themselves, for most of us, if we don't routinize evangelism, it will find little expression in our lives. There are simply too many things that will keep us busy and distract us. We will all spend eternity in worship and in deep conversations with friends and family; but this is the only time in our existence we will have the opportunity to participate in evangelism. It is too important to be left to chance.

Practice Evangelism until Evangelism Becomes Your Practice

We have made a practice of setting specific times aside for the purpose of evangelism. For example, we have people who go, weekly, to a local homeless mission here in Oklahoma City with the purpose of praying for people and leading them to Christ. Sometimes we set times for teams of people to go out to the neediest areas of our city and go door to door spreading the gospel and praying for people. We go to drug-ridden neighborhoods, bus stations, hospitals, and anywhere we can find people who are hungry and desperate for Jesus. We have seen incredible fruit and amazing testimonies of salvations and healings through these regularly scheduled times of intentional evangelism.

There are several advantages to scheduled times of evangelism. First, you can do it with your friends who are on the same faith journey as you. Together you can mutually encourage and debrief each other. You can discuss what worked and what didn't and learn and grow together.

Second, you gain faith and experience in an intentional way rather than waiting for spontaneous evangelistic opportunities. You get more comfortable with failure. You get used to hearing "no" to your offers of prayer without getting offended. You learn to hear and respond to the voice of God over the voice of fear. Then when you find yourself in a spontaneous moment of evangelism, you have a wealth of experience behind you to give you faith for what to say and what to pray.

Third, you learn how to live naturally supernatural. When you intentionally practice carrying the supernatural presence of

God into the streets, it fills you with faith to live a naturally supernatural daily life.

On the Streets of Oklahoma City

One afternoon, my friend Jim Kimbrough and I (Brian) decided to cruise around downtown Oklahoma City to look for opportunities to pray for people. We had set out that day with the purpose of practicing power evangelism. It wasn't long before we saw a man on crutches on a sidewalk. We pulled the car up beside him and hopped out of the car.

We approached the man, greeted him warmly and asked what had happened to get him into this condition. He shared with us that he was in a car accident and had to have his bones pinned together around the knee. He had about a six or seven pain level and very limited mobility, with about three-to-six inches in range.

We then told him why we pulled over and asked if we could pray for him. He agreed. After we prayed, we followed up and asked how his pain level was. He said it was about a three or four. We asked about his mobility. He could move his knee with much more range than he did before. By the time we finished, he had no pain and he was lifting his leg almost as far as you could. He actually left us walking across a field without the aid of crutches.

It is in moments like these that the kingdom draws near to the broken and hurting people God loves so much. It is also at these times of planned evangelism that we come to know the Father's heart for the lost and wounded. We gain a greater understanding of God's eagerness to touch people, and we also gain experience which sharpens our skills at evangelism.

A Day on Exchange Avenue

I mentioned in a previous chapter that I often go to an area in Oklahoma City on Exchange Avenue to practice power evangelism and demonstrate the love of Jesus and the reality of the kingdom of God. The reason I love this place so much is that it's an area which is largely forgotten by the church. It's an area that most proper Christians would avoid. Full of poverty, crime, addictions, and sickness, it's the type of place most of us like to pretend doesn't exist; but it's exactly the kind of place where I believe Jesus would hang out if He were here in the flesh today. The people there are hungry, but many of them are satisfying their hunger in destructive ways. The hungry are usually more likely to respond to a divine encounter with the living Christ than people living comfortable, suburban, middle and upper class lifestyles. It's a gritty place, but I love it.

Over the last several years, I have made a practice of going out to Exchange, and I usually bring a friend or two with me. I love to bring people who are new to power evangelism. It's a way to teach them the art by throwing them into the deep end. Because the people who live on Exchange are so hungry, it's a place where God often does some pretty amazing things. It's a great place to begin learning how to walk naturally supernaturally in power evangelism.

One Saturday, I took a team of four twenty-something women with me to Exchange. Our church had been hosting some power evangelism workshops, and these ladies were pretty excited (but also scared) about attempting to put into practice what they had learned. I was also pretty nervous. No matter how long you have been doing it, you still never know what will happen. I was especially nervous to be taking four young women into a pretty rough neighborhood.

There is never a comfortable way to approach people on the streets when doing intentional power evangelism, but what we have discovered is that, among hungry people like those on Exchange, it really doesn't matter how you approach them. If you can get the first sentence out of your mouth, you will either get the door slammed on you or something amazing will happen. The technique we were trying this day was a new one. We decided to go door-to-door being very bold and announcing that the kingdom of God was at hand right now.

We went to the first door and knocked. When someone came to the screen door, I said, "Excuse me. The kingdom of God is at hand…" (I'm positive I sounded like a complete nut.) "… and I would like to prove it to you. If you have any sickness in your body, God is going to heal you." We laid it on the line.

An older lady opened the door and let us in. She was using a cane. She said she had hurt her leg very badly, and her hip had also been injured two years before. "I'm in a lot of pain. I've been praying all night long for Jesus to heal me."

So Jesus showed up in answer to her prayer in the form of four young ladies and a fat guy. Who knew that the answer to her prayers would come this way! She called us angels. We prayed for her and released the kingdom of God on her. She experienced total relief from her pain, and we all praised God for touching her.

Her cane now sits in my office as a reminder of the healing that happened that day. She didn't want it anymore, so I decided to start a collection.

We left that lady's house with a testimony in our hands. We went door-to-door telling about the lady's healing. "See this cane? We took it from an old lady! She didn't need it anymore."

Nothing seemed to happen at the second door or the third. At one door, we were able to share a prophetic word with a woman, and she was significantly touched by the Lord.

As we moved on, we approached a lady who was putting laundry on a line. We showed her the cane and asked if we could pray for healing for anyone in the house. She responded, "My grandma is sick. She has diabetes and back pain."

"That's great! Can you go get her so we can pray for her?" (I always tend to get overly excited about people being sick. I've learned to see it as an opportunity for them to be healed.)

She went in the house and came back a moment later saying her grandmother was on the phone. We asked how long until she would be able to come out. She said her grandma might be on the phone for a couple of hours, so I asked, "Are the clothes on your line dry yet?" She said no. I asked her to go into the house and grab a towel. I explained how in the Bible people were healed through Paul's handkerchief. "Let's just believe that God can do something through the towel."

Here were four girls and I praying over a towel with an unbeliever. All of a sudden, a lady came out of the house and grabbed the towel with us and joined us in prayer. I stopped and asked her who she was and found out she was the sick grandma. "You don't need to pray over the towel. Let us pray for you."

We started telling her about some of the things that had already happened, and the four girls began to pray for her. Before we could even pray for her back, the lady started yelling that her back pain was gone. She felt heat all over her body. We asked if we could also pray for her diabetes.

I said, "I'm sure you already know about Jesus, but have you made Him king of your life? Have you given Him everything?" She said no. All of us went down on our knees, right there in the middle of the neighborhood with drug deals happening around us, and this lady was born again. Not bad for an hour and a half on a Saturday afternoon.

Routinization is important, not just to help us grow in evangelism and the exercise of spiritual gifts, but also for the people who encounter the love of God in a way that wouldn't have been possible without our obedience to go. Maybe there's a place like Exchange where you live, where people are hungry and desperate, and where God is leading you to start your evangelism routine. It doesn't really matter whether you go to urban slums, suburban coffee shops, or rural markets. Just start somewhere and trust the Lord to lead you and teach you along the way.

Insight Nine: Press Through the Pushback

Our challenge is to understand the nature of the conflict and then fight with the weapons God has given us, always keeping our focus on Him.

Dianna and I (Charles) were walking through the streets of Zurich, Switzerland, with our friends, Richard and Lora Clinton. We had ministered the previous evening in the young church Richard was pastoring. We had experienced an outpouring of the Holy Spirit, with a number of people receiving physical healing. Zurich this Monday morning was in the midst of a carnival; the streets were crowded and there was a festive mood in the air. Out of the crowd a man made his way to my wife and I, and he began taunting and insulting us. He was nose to nose with me, spewing one insult after another. I was alarmed and taken aback. This was not the nature of the peace-loving Swiss I knew. We began to walk away, and he walked alongside of us, continuing with the insults. Because of the festivities of the morning, one had to watch where one stepped because there was horse dung on the streets. The man insulting us stepped right into a pile; he smiled and said "delightful." I found myself growing angrier and angrier with this man's continued insults.

And then out of this man's mouth came, "This is my country! I have been here for hundreds of years. You have no right to be here! Get out of my country!" Then he turned on a dime and quickly melted back into the crowd. The hair on my arms stood up. We stood there stunned with the dawning awareness that we were talking to more than a rude citizen; we were confronted by a spiritual being who had taken notice of the in-breaking of the kingdom of God the previous evening. It should not surprise us that whenever we move out to expand the kingdom of God, we should expect the enemy to notice.

There is a War

The Apostle Paul writes in Ephesians 6:12:

For our struggle is not against flesh and blood, but against the rulers, against the authorities, against the powers of this dark world and against the spiritual forces in the heavenly realms.

We are in a battle; there are malevolent spiritual beings that wish to keep the world in darkness trying to do us harm.

Evangelism puts us on the front line. The problem with much of western Christianity is that many of us do not seem to know there is a war going on. When seeking to advance the kingdom of God, conflict is to be expected. Those without a saving knowledge of Christ, those well-intentioned Christians who speak ill of us, and those of other faith traditions are never our enemy. The god of this world who has blinded the minds of unbelievers is our enemy (2 Corinthians 4:4). In the words of John Wimber, "Satan is our *ultimate* enemy, but not our *immediate* enemy."

Those engaged in advancing the kingdom of God don't have to look for conflict. Conflict will find them. As we announce and demonstrate that the kingdom of God is at hand, we will experience resistance from time to time. Some of this resistance may be institutional as we move against the dominant culture of pluralism. Some of the resistance may be personal as those we are ministering to are made uncomfortable by our boldness. At times, the resistance will be internal, because we must confront our own shyness and fear of appearing foolish.

Jesus Experienced Pushback

Immediately after Jesus' baptism, He was led into the wilderness where He was tempted by the devil. From there, He returned to Galilee in the power of the Holy Spirit. While many welcomed His message and ministry, there were others who resisted Him. Those in His own hometown of Capernaum were furious with Him and literally drove Him out of the town with the expressed purpose of killing Him (Luke 4:28-29). The religious leaders grew angry with Jesus and began to plot His demise when He healed on the Sabbath (Luke 6:11). They even attributed His ministry to the power of Beelzebub (Mark 3:22).

Jesus' own family failed to understand His ministry and at one point, "they went to take charge of him, for they said, 'He is out of his mind'" (Mark 3:21). He even received pushback from some of His closest associates. Peter was inspired by Satan to rebuke Jesus and dissuade Jesus from His mission, and Judas was moved by Satan to betray Jesus. In the Garden of Gethsemane, Jesus "began to be sorrowful and troubled." He said to His closest disciples, "My soul is overwhelmed with sorrow to the point of death," and out of this pain He prayed repeatedly, "My Father, if it is possible, may this cup [of suffering] be taken from me" (Matthew 26:36-43). Luke records that in response to this prayer God sent an angel to strengthen Jesus (Luke 22:43).

Jesus experienced spiritual, family, religious, relational, and even internal pushback, and we can expect the same. Some of the pushback will come from well meaning people, but some of it will be demonically motivated. As with Jesus, the enemy will seek to work through our family, friends, religious systems, and secular institutions. We also have the added weakness of our personal brokenness and appetite for sin. We must receive and actively live in the empowerment of the Holy Spirit. It is in our intimacy with God that we find the strength, wisdom and insight to understand the enemy's schemes and activities.

We are to Expect Suffering

Pushback always involves suffering. The apostle Peter writes (I'm sure from personal experience) that we must:

> Be self-controlled and alert. Your enemy the devil prowls around like a roaring lion looking for someone to devour. Resist him, standing firm in the faith, because you know that your brothers throughout the world are undergoing the same kind of sufferings. (1 Peter 5:8-9)

Jesus didn't come to give us a life free from suffering. He came to bring us back into right relationship with the Father and give us eternal life. We serve a God who was beaten and hung on a tree. He wasn't esteemed, and as His disciples, we should expect that following in His footsteps will generate opposition as well. The question isn't whether or not we will experience suffering and conflict as a result of pursuing the kingdom ministry of Jesus, but rather what we will do with it when it comes. Will our response be to step back into the safety of powerless living, or will we press through the pushback?

Some dear friends of ours, Josh and Nancy Kouri, experienced a huge pushback from the enemy a couple of years ago. Josh is a pastor on the front lines of ministry, doing powerful things in the kingdom of God to see the lost saved in Oklahoma City. Everything in his life seemed to be going well until one day his son, Elijah became deathly ill. Elijah went from healthy and vibrant one day to being admitted to a pediatric ICU the next. His life literally hung in the balance. His chances of survival were slim, and doctors believed that in the unlikely event that he did survive, he would need long-term rehabilitation and carry lasting effects of the illness the rest of his life.

Faced with the precarious uncertainty of their son's life and future, Josh and Nancy were obviously devastated. They fought against encroaching despair. Friends, family, and church members would come and pray with them during the day, but at night, fear and anguish would abound. They decided to focus their thoughts and heart on the Lord and His sufficiency. They found strength in the Psalms and in worship. They fought against the despair by speaking truth about the goodness and supremacy of God, the truth of Scriptures, and words and promises spoken over their son. In the midst of the onslaught, they took refuge in the Lord, hiding under the shadow of His wings.

I (Brian) would go to visit Josh and Nancy regularly to pray over Elijah. In the midst of their seemingly hopeless situation, Josh and Nancy fought back by continuing to do the work of the kingdom. While his son was hooked up to machines in the pediatric ICU, Josh grabbed me aside and asked me to go with him to pray for other patients on the floor. He chose to battle the encroaching fear and despair by focusing on Christ and His mission, reaching out to others in need. He and Nancy continued praying for all the other patients and their families around them. Even though they were facing mounting medical expenses, I saw them moving in a spirit of generosity, giving to others in need in spite of their own situation.

Elijah did make a full recovery. It was truly a miracle! Not only did he survive, but he did not need any on-going care and has had no lasting effects from the illness. By the time he was released from the hospital, Josh and Nancy had prayed for and ministered to many others in need. All the other people on the floor had been touched by God through Josh's family, some of them able to leave the hospital early because of God's healing touch. In the midst of struggle and pushback from the enemy, Josh and Nancy were not being pushed back, they were pressing through.

Counting the Cost

I (Brian) have struggled greatly with the warfare that comes with a life committed to advancing the kingdom of God. The pushback comes to different people in different ways. My biggest struggle has come in the form of assaulting and tormenting thoughts. The enemy comes at me strongly with accusation, condemnation, and fear—tactics meant not only to destroy me, but to keep me from advancing the kingdom of God. If the enemy can get me to stop looking to Jesus and begin looking at myself and the mental warfare, then he not only takes me out, but he effectively prevents me from touching the lives of others and seeing them come into their destinies in God.

Over the years in which I have been stepping out in power evangelism, I have struggled with depression, anxiety, sleeplessness, and the physical problems that come with them. During my early twenties, the problems became so severe that I had to seek professional help in order to function. At one of the lowest points I can remember, I was having such difficulty with depression and tormenting thoughts that a friend of mine who is a Christian counselor suggested I might need to meet with a psychiatrist colleague of hers to evaluate if there was a chemical problem that needed to be treated medically. So there I sat in a sterile office, face-to-face with a psychiatrist who didn't know me, feeling so vulnerable and discouraged that I was longing to get out of the room. In an attempt to diagnose my condition, the psychiatrist was barraging me with questions. At one point he asked, "Do you hear voices?"

I wasn't sure how to answer that. I'd hear the Holy Spirit speak to me, and at times, in the midst of the battle, I could clearly hear the voice of the enemy as well. Would this psychiatrist understand if I tried to explain this, or would I just sound insane? At that point, I wasn't entirely sure I wasn't insane. It all seemed very confusing in my mind. I timidly replied, "Yes, but not the kind of voices you are talking about."

Words can't describe how low this moment was for me. But then, right in the middle of my deepest moment of despair, I heard God speak to me. I suddenly began to get a download from God of words of knowledge for this psychiatrist. On the one hand, I was filled with hope and consolation knowing that Jesus was right there with me, speaking to me, at my darkest moment. He hadn't abandoned me. He was with me. On the other hand, I had no idea what to do with those impressions. If I shared them, would the psychiatrist think I was even more crazy? I was bewildered. I decided not to say anything.

After my session was finally over, I went to my counselor's office and told her what had happened. I shared the words of knowledge with her, and she was glad that I hadn't said anything to the psychiatrist. She told me it would have freaked him out and he wouldn't have known what to do, but she offered to go share the words with him herself. She later met with the psychiatrist and said, "You know that guy Brian? I know he's got problems, but he really does hear from God. This is what God spoke to him about you." She went on to share the words of knowledge I had received. He acknowledged that all of them were true. As it turned out, the man was in the midst of a personal crisis himself, and he wasn't a believer. I was in the middle of my own crisis, feeling intense pushback. In the midst of my crisis, God was speaking to me, bringing consolation to me, and at the same time He was using what the enemy meant for evil to destroy me to bring life and healing to both me and the psychiatrist.

The pushback will come. For me it comes as depression, anxiety, and fear. For you it may come in a different form such as isolationism, complacency, busy living, fleshly temptation, or any number of things. I have learned that the challenge is to rest in God's love, trust in His goodness and sufficiency, and battle the thoughts from the position of resting in Christ rather than out of my own strength or desperation. I had to learn to take every thought captive to make it obedient to Christ (2 Corinthians 10:5) and be transformed by the renewing of my mind (Romans 12:2). I had to learn to live out of the love of God for me rather than out of the fear and intimidation the enemy dished out to me. It's a daily struggle, and one I'm still battling. There is a cost to be counted for advancing the kingdom, but we are never without comfort. We are never powerless against the enemy. We must learn to fix our eyes on Christ and commit our lives to advancing the kingdom and pursuing His love for us and others no matter the cost.

Chips, Dips and Kingdom Conflict

Let me give you a typical example of what the enemy's pushback can look like for me. One day I went to lunch at a Mexican restaurant with my friend Paul. We were just hanging out, eating chips and salsa, talking about life and minding our own business. I noticed a couple come into the restaurant. They were very beautiful and healthy looking. They looked like they could be personal trainers. But when I looked at the man, a picture came through my mind about a ministry encounter I had before. The memory of a word of knowledge I had about a guy's back at a restaurant popped back into my mind. This memory came as a fleeting, still small voice while I was eating my chips and dip. I knew from experience that God was giving me a word of knowledge for this man about a problem in his back.

Immediately after this, a barrage of dark thoughts came to my mind. *You're just making this up. You're just trying to show off in front of Paul. If you get up and share this, the guy is just going to laugh at you and you're going to feel embarrassed.* Other thoughts, condemning thoughts, kept pelting my mind. All I was doing was hanging out with my friend, enjoying my chips and dip, and the thought came to me about this guy's back. My initial thought, though faint, was clear and filled me with faith and curiosity. But then came the onslaught of fiery darts pelting my mind—accusations and disqualifications along with a good dose of fear and intimidation.

Oftentimes, when there is an opportunity to advance the kingdom of God, some kind of internal conflict like this arises which we *must* push through. The enemy's agenda is to keep us from stepping out to release the presence and power of the kingdom. He will try to question and pervert what God is speaking to us. Here is how we can often recognize the difference between his voice and the voice of the Spirit: when the Spirit of God is speaking, it is often a still, small voice. It is almost like a fleeting thought, but there is faith and excitement in it. The enemy's voice, on the other hand, is filled with harassment and bullying thoughts that accuse and condemn and attempt to put fear in us.

On the outside, my friend Paul probably never knew about this spiritual battle going on inside me. I had two options. I could either go with the first impression I had received, or I could shut down and listen to these other thoughts. This is what I did in that moment: I simply prayed, *Holy Spirit, I believe you were speaking to me about this guy's back, but I have all this other stuff going on. Can you please give me some other information as a sign that this is you?*

I thought it was kind of funny when the waiter sat the couple right behind me so that the man's back was right up against my back. Even as I felt the Lord was assuring me with this sign, the thoughts from the enemy didn't let up. In fact, they increased more.

I simply asked, *Holy Spirit, would you give me another sign?* This time, I felt a pain shoot up and down my back. Again, the harassment and fear came: *You're going to look stupid now. You are going to embarrass yourself and your friend.* This persisted, so I asked the Lord to give me more information about this man and the woman with him. Then I felt like I started getting information about their character and who they were. Again, the onslaught of the enemy came on even stronger. Fear was rising up, but I was determined to press through it.

I said to Paul, "Excuse me for a second. I think God might be speaking to me about these people." I turned and went to their table.

"I'm sorry to interrupt your lunch, but sometimes God speaks to me and gives me pictures and impressions about people. Do you mind if I take a minute to share what I got?"

They both looked at one another with that "this is weird" look I have come to expect. Then they said "Okay."

I just began to share with the man the things I saw as attributes and characteristics of his life. I asked if it made sense, and he said yes. So then I turned to the lady and began to tell her that she was very business-minded and had a tenacious personality. I told her that she had an entrepreneurial spirit. I asked if this made sense, and she said it did. I also told her that she had been having trouble sleeping at night, and she was having problems with depression, very up and down feelings. I also pointed out that she was having female problems, and she had been concerned for some time. She nervously looked at her friend and said all of this was correct.

Then I turned to the man and told him, "You have been having problems in your back for some time now. It happened because of a sporting accident a long time ago. Is that true?" He said he had been having back problems ever since he was injured it as a young boy playing football. They both looked at each other and then at me with that "this is *really* weird" look. I said, "May I simply pray for you? I know we are at the restaurant, and I don't want to embarrass you. But God wouldn't speak to me about these things if He didn't want to do something about them."

It's always funny when this happens, because you never know what the reaction of the people will be. I guess this couple now thought they were in church because they reverently closed their eyes and bowed their heads and allowed me to pray for them.

After I prayed, I simply said, "The reason Jesus showed this to me was because He wants you to know that He is actively pursuing you. He knows exactly where you are in life, and His love is extended toward you." I didn't feel like I needed to go any further. I felt like that was all I needed to share. Normally I would give an invitation for them to be born again and give their lives to Jesus, but, for some reason, I felt that was all I was to say. I thanked them for allowing me to interrupt their lunch, and Paul and I grabbed our ticket and left.

Right after this encounter I said, *Lord thank you for speaking and allowing me to give this message to this couple.*

Immediately, warfare began to pelt my mind once again. *I can't believe you didn't lead that guy to Jesus. You messed the whole thing up. You're a loser.* The Lord showed me that day that the enemy works to abort the movement of the Spirit from the beginning, the middle, and the end. He comes to steal, and he wants to kill you and me in the process.

Press Through by Focusing on Christ

How are we to fight and press through the pushback? The writer of Hebrews states:

> *Therefore, since we are surrounded by such a great cloud of witnesses, let us throw off everything that hinders and the sin that so easily entangles. And let us run with perseverance the race marked out for us, **fixing our eyes on Jesus**, the pioneer and perfecter of faith. For the joy set before him he endured the cross, scorning its shame, and sat down at the right hand of the throne of God. **Consider him who endured such opposition from sinners, so that you will not grow weary and lose heart.***
> *(Hebrews 12:1-3, emphasis added)*

We press through the pushback by fixing our eyes on Jesus, considering Him so that we will not grow weary and lose heart. As we focus on Jesus, the intimidation rising from the enemy's tactics fades in comparison with the glory of Christ. We remember that our weapons are not of this world but involve setting our thoughts in line with heaven's thoughts (2 Corinthians 10:4-5). We fight by resting in the love of God for us. From the place of rest the Lord fights our battles for us.

The enemy's tactics are designed to distract, confuse, and distort. His schemes are designed to strip you of your identity and rob you of your calling. His goal is to get you on the defensive, getting you to focus your attention on his strategies. We cannot live in reaction to the strategies of hell. If we do, we have lost, because our focus is no longer on Christ and His mission; but as we fix our eyes firmly on Christ, we remain aligned with the purposes and strategies of heaven.

A couple of years ago, I (Brian) had a vision. It was like a movie playing out in my mind. The first scene was of a man who was going about life when suddenly a huge number of large, black hornets began to swarm around his head, flying at him from every direction. He began to swat at the hornets, trying to get them off him. He was becoming frantic and afraid. As the man was distracted by the swarm of hornets, he didn't realize that a large black spider was descending upon his head. The spider landed on his head and began to weave a web all over the top of his head. Next I saw a person come up behind the man and cut the back of his hair off. The scene switched and I saw the same man. He was lying down on the ground. He had been taken captive and tied up by a bunch of little men, just like in the book *Gulliver's Travels*. I saw this vision in my mind's eye, but I didn't have any understanding with it.

Then the Lord immediately showed me the vision again, but this time I understood. Again I saw the man, and the hornets began to swarm him. I understood that this was how the onslaught of the enemy works. He brings pelting thoughts from every direction. The man was distracted by this attack from the enemy. While he was distracted and afraid, he didn't realize that the enemy was weaving a web of deceit in his mind (the spider weaving the web on his head). His mind was now full of the cobwebs of confusion and doubt. In this fearful and confused state, the enemy was able to come and steal his strength, represented by cutting his hair off.

Then I saw the second scene, again, of the man lying on the ground, bound by the little people; but this time I saw the scene differently. What I thought had been ropes or chains holding the man were not that at all. I looked at the little bitty people and saw they held cans of silly string. The man was being held down by nothing but silly string. Then I heard the Lord say to me, "They are just little bitty lies. It's only silly string. You can just get up. 'Arise and shine for your light has come!' (Isaiah 60:1)."

Over the following months and now years, the Lord has continued to speak to me through this vision. The lies and schemes of the enemy may seem to overwhelm me, but I can simply arise, get up, and shake them off. It is because of Christ, the Light who has come, that we are able to overcome the onslaught of the enemy's attacks. As we focus on Him, our Light, we can arise and stand in who we are through Him and live in the calling and destiny He has sovereignly given us.

The pushback will come, but we must never begin to doubt that Satan is a defeated foe. There is no question about how this spiritual war will end. We rest in the work Christ has already accomplished on our behalf, fix our eyes only on Him, and allow Him to fight the battles for us.

Press Through With Prayer

When we are experiencing pushback, we must also recognize the spiritual dimension of this conflict and engage in spiritual warfare through prayer. Part of our praying is defensive as we ask God for protection for ourselves and those we love. We ask Him to help us as we seek first His kingdom. Before Jesus' betrayal, in the Garden of Gethsemane, Jesus prayed and was given strength to carry out God's will (Luke 22:42-44). Likewise, when we engage in spiritual warfare, we seek God's help to strengthen us for the battle and keep us in His care.

Another part of our praying is offensively minded, being directed against the demonic strongholds in our area as we invite the kingdom of God to come and be established. As we engage in prayer in this way, we often become aware of the enemy's tactics and are able to combat them. As the Holy Spirit gives us insight into the enemy's activities we can move forward with God's power and wisdom.

Press Through with Scripture

We also press through the pushback using Scripture. The Word of God is a powerful weapon against the enemy's schemes. As darkness comes to us with opposition, temptation, and oppression, we can rely on the truth of God's Word to lead us. It is through Scripture that we come to know who God is, who we are, and how we are to live. The enemy comes at us with lies and half-truths. As we know the truth found in Scripture and hide it in our hearts, it becomes a beacon, illuminating the truth and exposing the enemy's tactics.

In Matthew 4, when Jesus was led into the wilderness after His baptism, He experienced a huge pushback from the enemy. It was here that Satan leveled his best shot at Jesus in an attempt to abort the mission of God before His ministry even began. Jesus could have responded in many ways, but in all three instances, Jesus combated Satan's assaults with Scripture. The Word of God is living and active, sharper than any double-edged sword (Hebrews 4:12). As we spend time in the Word of God, allowing it to penetrate us and transform us, it becomes a powerful weapon against the attacks of the enemy.

Press Through by Giving out of Your Need

In Acts 5:12-42, we find the apostles boldly proclaiming the gospel in Jerusalem, healing the sick, and performing miracles. This enraged the powers of darkness, and the apostles were all arrested and placed in prison. While awaiting their fate, an angel came to them in prison, released them and commanded them to go right back out on the streets and tell the people about the new life they had found in Jesus. They did so, only to be confronted by the Sanhedrin and flogged. Even after this, they continually shared the gospel everywhere they went, from the temple courts to people's homes. The pushback was extreme, yet they didn't allow it to deter them from their mission.

There are times when the pushback can feel overwhelming. In these times, it would be easy to want to withdraw and stop living a life on a mission for the kingdom of God. While it is vitally important that we have a rhythm in place in which we find solace and strength in the sanctuary, we cannot remain there. There are times when the best way to combat the enemy's attacks is by steeling ourselves with resolve to continue in a life on a mission, trusting in God's goodness despite how we feel. Even in our times of greatest need, the Holy Spirit desires to move through us to reach those around us. When we find ourselves in need, we give of ourselves out of our place of need, empowered by the Holy Spirit. It is at our weakest points that our dependence upon Him is greatest. It is in our weakness that we are strong (2 Corinthians 12:10).

I (Brian) recently faced a very difficult time in my life. I was at a point of burnout. I had become over-stressed by taking on a position as a staff pastor and elder in our church, while still maintaining my business, and at the same time I was a husband and father to six young children, including two-year-old triplets. My life had become filled with stress, depression, and anxiety as

I tried my best to hear from God what I was to do next. I had come to a place where I realized that it was necessary for me to take a sabbatical from pastoring. The depression, fear, and anxiety were overwhelming. It was being topped off with a good dose of confusion and accusation from the enemy. I felt like I had failed God, my family, and the church.

I walked into my office at the church where I saw my intern, Matt Burrell. Matt has a heart and hunger for God, and he has devoted his life to advancing the kingdom of God. Part of the reason he had taken on the internship was his desire to learn from me and grow in the area of healing. I had to tell him I would not be on the church staff any longer, at least for quite a while. I asked him to join me for a ride in my car so I could break the news to him and explain my reasons. As we talked, I found myself driving to the area around Exchange Avenue. It was unintentional at first, but then I began to sense the Holy Spirit's direction. I began to get very clear instruction: turn here, go straight, turn there, now go to those apartments and knock on that particular door.

I parked the car and we got out. Matt asked, "What are we doing here?"

I cryptically said, "You'll see." I didn't know what we were doing either, but I knew it would be good because the Holy Spirit was orchestrating it.

I walked up to the door the Holy Spirit had directed me to and knocked. An older lady answered, standing behind her screen door. I introduced myself saying, "Hi, my name is Brian and this is Matt. We are followers of Jesus. We were in the area, and we wanted to see if anyone here has any needs we could pray for." She didn't really respond. I didn't have any kind of word of knowledge to share, no direction for what to do next, just a confidence that God wanted to do something here. "Is anybody sick? Any blood conditions? Any back pain?" I listed off several things.

"Yeah, I have a back problem that causes me pain."

"Really? How bad is the back pain right now on a scale from one to ten, ten being the worst?" She said it was around a seven or an eight.

She was talking to us from behind her screen door which she hadn't offered to open. I sensed that to ask her to either come out on the porch with us or to open the door and let us come in might make her feel very uncomfortable. So I said, "Put your hand on the screen door, and I will put my hand on the screen as well. I'm going to ask the Holy Spirit to come, and His presence is going to come upon you and heal you."

Matt and I began to pray for her. We paused to ask her what she was experiencing. She said she felt warmth on her back and the pain was decreasing. I now felt it was appropriate to ask her if she would be comfortable coming out on the porch so we could pray some more.

"Yes, but wait a minute." She motioned inside the house to someone else. It was a younger friend of hers, and both the ladies came out with us on the porch.

I turned to the younger girl and said, "You are going to help us pray for your friend." She had a bewildered look on her face, and before she had the chance to fully process what I was saying and back out, I told her, "Put your hand on your friend's back and watch as the presence of God comes. He will complete this healing through you." I told her to ask the Holy Spirit to come. She looked confused, so I told her to just repeat after me. "Holy Spirit, let your power come." She repeated my words.

Both ladies became wide-eyed with shock and amazement as each of them sensed something happening. I asked them what was going on.

The older lady said with shock, "The pain is gone."

The young girl was staring at her hand, clearly freaked out by what had just happened. I asked, "You could feel that, couldn't you? You felt power coming out of your hand." She said yes and kept nodding her head, totally astounded at what she had just experienced. I explained, "The reason why you felt that in your hand is because Jesus said the kingdom of God is at hand, meaning His presence is near and tangible."

Matt and I talked with them there on the porch, helping them understand what they had just experienced. We shared the gospel with them. I explained, "Jesus did this because He is close and near you. He wants a relationship with you."

I was sensing something for the younger lady, so I shared it. "You have been vacillating between two lives, and the Lord wants you to know He loves you and is near you. Later this evening when you are lying in bed, ask the presence of God to come, and I believe He will." We shared with them a little longer and left.

This entire encounter was amazing to me: not so much because of the healing testimony, but because of what was going on inside of me. I had started out that day utterly dejected, feeling like a failure because I was stepping down from a formal ministry position. I was weak and felt I had absolutely nothing left to give. I was mentally, physically, and spiritually exhausted, in acute need of healing and renewal myself. I felt exposed, and the enemy was assaulting my thoughts with accusation, condemnation, rejection, and fear. It was in that very weak moment that God assured me of what I needed to hear most: He wasn't done with me yet. As I partnered with Him to minister to these two ladies, I also felt the Lord ministering to me, assuring me that He had a plan for me, a plan to prosper me and give me a future and a hope (Jeremiah 29:11).

We must learn to be content knowing that we are imperfect, yet He desires to bring about His perfect plans through us. As followers of Jesus going through a progressive process of becoming more like Him, we walk around as living contradictions. Full of faith one minute, full of doubt the next. Confident in our identity in Christ one minute, overcome by fear the next. God isn't afraid of the contradictions. His desire is to bring to the surface those lingering doubts and fears so that they can be dealt with as He transforms us into the image of His Son. When they do come to the surface, the enemy often assaults us with condemnation, fear, temptation, and despair. Our job is to recognize that we are in a battle and stand firm in our faith, as Paul admonishes us in Ephesians 6:10-17. The pushback will come, but it does not have to overcome us. We can press through the pushback and into the destiny God has for us.

Insight Ten: The "How" Is Just as Important as the "What"

Our challenge is to think and pray through a set of biblical ministry values and seek to integrate them into our life and practice.

People may not receive God's healing, but they can always receive our love. The way we approach ministry, the way we treat the people we are ministering to, our own sense of responsibility for the outcome of the ministry time, and how we are to help people process their disappointment when nothing seems to happen are all built upon a set of values.

Values are basic assumptions we make about how we should do life. From our values we develop a set of priorities. Priorities are what we focus our time, attention, and resources toward. Our values and priorities give shape to our practices.

I (Charles) grew up, the oldest of five children. Our home was always a place we felt comfortable bringing our friends and it was not unusual to find many of the neighborhood kids at our house. (My mother would sometimes complain, "Don't your friends have homes you can visit?") We would play in our bedrooms and hangout in the living room watching TV while my mom offered us snacks. My father was enlisted in the Air Force, and I lived much of my early life on Air Force bases where all the houses were basically the same.

One of my close friends, who was an only child, invited me into his house while he ran in to grab his baseball mitt. To my surprise, when I stepped through the front door, I was told not to proceed by his mother and to wait for my friend by the doorway. There was a plastic runner that ran over the carpet and through the living room. The furniture was covered with clear plastic wrap. Even the lamps were covered in plastic. I stood there in shock and amazement. I wondered, *How could anyone have fun in this house?*

My friend returned from his bedroom with his baseball mitt and we made our way to an open field to join a newly-forming baseball game. On the way to the field, I asked my friend about his house and about all the plastic I saw. He explained that his parents liked to entertain other adults and his mother insisted on the furniture looking nice.

We both lived in houses that looked the same on the outside, but our mothers had very different sets of values and priorities. These values set the tone and atmosphere within our respected homes. Rough and frayed around the edges, kid-friendly furniture verses pristine showcase furniture reflected our parents' values and priorities.

With my own family of six children, my wife and I struggle with that tension of having a teenage-friendly home and having really nice furniture that will stay nice. We presently have three sons still living at home, one college freshman and two college students who are also members of a rock band that practices in a converted garage that serves as an extra bedroom. It is not unusual for a dozen or so young people to be hanging out at our house at any given time. (I sometimes find myself telling my own sons, "Don't your friends have homes you can visit?")

Values not only shape the way we decorate our homes and who we let in, values also shape our ministry priorities and practices. Two different churches can emphasize praying for the sick, but their values can cause the same ministry to look totally different. The following are some of the values that shape our approach to ministry and the people we minister to.

God is Actively Involved in and with His Creation

We know that we covered this in insight three, "God Is Always at Work around Us," but it bears repeating. Because we believe that God is already involved in people's lives, this takes the pressure off of us to make anything happen. God is already intimately doing something in them. Our job is to ask the Father what He is doing and how he wants us to cooperate with His present activity. We simply respond with faith and obedience to whatever He shows us.

God Loves People

God loves broken people. God loves sick people. God loves religious people. God loves people who do not yet love Him back. Love is not simply something that God does; love is His very nature and character.

God does not turn away from sinners in disgust, He moves toward them with compassion and grace. The parable of the prodigal son is as much about the love and character of God as it is about repentance on behalf of the younger brother. It is a tremendous privilege to minister to people because they are the object of God's love and affection.

Being God-Focused Rather than Sin-Focused

Gregory Boyd opens up his book *Repenting of Religion* with a story of himself sitting in a mall on a Saturday afternoon, sipping a Coke, watching people as they pass by. Soon his people watching turned into people judging as he began to make judgments on the basis of what people wore, their facial expressions, how they related to others, and so on. He found himself concluding that some were godly while others were not. As he recognized what he was doing, he also realized that he felt good while doing it. Boyd even goes so far as to say this activity of judging others was feeding him.[10]

This issue of examining what is feeding our soul is at the heart of learning to be God focused rather than sin focused. It is too easy to look at someone and make quick, and many times wrong, assumptions about why the person is sick, poor, or in the sorry condition he finds himself in. Our aim is not to try to figure out why the person is suffering. Rather, our aim is to ask God what He wants us to do. Jesus modeled this value throughout His ministry. He often spent his time with sinners, tax collectors, and prostitutes. Rather than focusing on the outward negative things we may notice about a person, ask God what He is doing and minister to him accordingly.

Dependence on the Holy Spirit and Not on Formulas

The Holy Spirit brings to us the power to do what only God can do at the moment of need. Magic operates under the assumption that the world is simply a force or set of physical or spiritual laws which can be manipulated. We are not shamans looking for the religious formulas that will unlock spiritual power; we are disciples of Christ, wholly dependent on God to give us grace at our point of need.

It is the Holy Spirit who empowers us to do ministry. We can only do what He empowers us to do in the moment, and there are times when we don't even know what that might be. Rather than conjuring up some religious platitudes, when we don't know what the Holy Spirit is doing, we can never go wrong with just listening to people and loving them.

Compassion and Kindness

As our friend Jack Moraine is fond of saying, "We may not be able to minister healing, but we can always minister love." We believe in treating everyone with compassion and kindness. Jesus tells us plainly that when we show kindness "to the least," He takes it personally. When we show kindness to people we are showing kindness toward God (Matthew 25:31-46).

Honesty and Truthfulness

It is not enough for us that a person has all the symptoms of his sickness, but claims "by faith to be healed." Our definition of healing says that the symptoms are gone or have subsided to a noticeable degree. If the person's condition is noticeably improved or totally gone, this is a victory. Our aim is to discern and bring healing to the root cause of the illness as well as alleviate the symptoms.

All healing is partial and temporary. All those whom Jesus healed eventually died. Even Lazarus who was raised from the dead returned back to the grave. None of us are totally well or healthy on this side of heaven. We live in the "now and not yet" reality of the kingdom.

We encourage those we minister to to be truthful about the measure of healing (if any) they have received, and we seek to be accurate when sharing these stories with others. Being truthful is a higher priority than being positive and less than truthful.

No Hype

It is important to us not to hype ministry, to make it seem bigger or more exciting than it really is. To us, faith must be rooted in reality and truthfulness, not wishful thinking.

Emotional excitement does not equal biblical faith, and neither does stretching the truth. We are not against the genuine release of emotion in response to the Holy Spirit's ministry, but we are against manipulation and stirring up emotions and calling this faith. The truth does not have to be hyped or supported by wishful thinking. No hype means we don't promise more than we can deliver, and we don't stretch or deny the truth in the name of building faith. Ministry must always be grounded in integrity.

Ministry is a Privilege

To minister as God's ambassador is a responsibility, but let us never forget that to minister God's grace to others is always a privilege. When we begin treating people as objects of our ministry or even worse, sources of income or affirmation, we are skating on thin ice. People are so important to God that Jesus was sent to die for them so that they could live forever with Him. To be given the opportunity to partner with God as He pours out His grace and mercy is an honor beyond what any of us deserve. If ministry becomes a burden and we become impatient with those Jesus loves and died for, we need to back up and reconnect with God.

Ministry Models Must be Reproducible

One of the things that continues to amaze us about Jesus is that He chose to do ministry in such a way that His disciples learned to do what He did. Jesus was very intentional about this.

He appointed twelve—designating them apostles—that they might be with him and that he might send them out to preach and to have authority to drive out demons. (Mark 3:14-15)

We believe that we are to be just as intentional as Jesus. Our goal in training others is to do ministry in a way that leaves them believing they can also do what we do. We know we have been successful when we quit being invited back to a church because they are not only doing empowered ministry, they are equipping others as well. Our goal is to work ourselves out of a job. '

We are always asking ourselves if the ministry models we are using are reproducible. If not, we try to figure out how to adjust how we do ministry so that others can feel empowered and equipped to do ministry as well. Again, we see this value expressed in the way Jesus did ministry, and we believe it must undergird what we do as well. Our job is not to build our ministry, it is to train and equip others to do the ministry of Christ.

Spiritual Authority is Based on My Relationship to Christ, Not My Own Goodness

Our authority to minister has been delegated to us by Jesus. We believe holiness is important, but our goodness is not the basis of our power. It rests in Christ and in Him alone. When we look to our own goodness (however we may define this) as the source of our power we are setting ourselves up for failure. We will either become a religious legalist if we feel we are good enough to minister, or if we are always falling short, we will feel disqualified. We minister out of God's love and His authority, not our goodness.

Team Ministry

Ministry is meant to be rooted in community. Jesus, upon being released and empowered to begin ministry, began by recruiting a team to work with Him. This was part of the fabric of His ministry. When Jesus sent His disciples out to minister, He did not send them to minster alone; He sent them out in pairs. There is protection in ministering alongside someone else. There is also encouragement and support. Ministry is refined in the context of a community of faith.

Proverbs 13:20 says, "He who walks with the wise grows wise." We will become like the people we spend time with. It is important to develop mentoring relationships with people wanting to do the ministry you are doing. We make it our practice to try to always bring along an apprentice to help us. Our intention is to reproduce our ministry practice and values in those we are training. Ministry is best taught when it is caught.

We are Both the Missionary and the Mission Field

Throughout our lives, God never stops working in our own hearts, exposing the areas that are hurt, hardened and resistant to Him. While we carry out Jesus' commission on the earth, we are also to continue to let God shape and mold us. We are simultaneously the missionary and the mission field.

Fortunately, we don't have to wait to be perfect to minister to others. On this side of eternity, we will always carry with us some degree of brokenness. We are not disqualified from ministry for being broken; however, losing sight of the fact that we are still a work in progress decreases our effectiveness in ministry. We approach ministry with humility: we realize our own need and lack, and in the midst of weakness we accept the grace available to join Jesus in His mission on the earth to bring greater glory to Him.

The Supremacy of Love

All ministry models are built on assumptions and values. Ministry built on wrong assumptions and non-biblical values can ultimately be harmful and detrimental to the work of the kingdom. The correct ministry done in a manipulative manner carries the seeds of corruption and confusion. It brings harm to all involved, to those being ministered to, and ultimately to the one doing the ministry as well. Paul makes this clear in the first few verses of 1 Corinthians 13, in which he describes love as the fundamental value that is to be imbedded in all ministry activity.

> *If I speak in the tongues of men and of angels, but have not love, I am only a resounding gong or a clanging cymbal. If I have the gift of prophecy and can fathom all mysteries and all knowledge, and if I have a faith that can move mountains, but have not love, I am nothing. If I give all I possess to the poor and surrender my body to the flames, but have not love, I gain nothing.*

> *Love is patient, love is kind. It does not envy, it does not boast, it is not proud. It is not rude, it is not self-seeking, it is not easily angered, it keeps no record of wrongs. Love does not delight in evil but rejoices with the truth. It always protects, always trusts, always hopes, always perseveres. (1 Corinthians 13:1-7)*

When we operate in the power and gifting of the Holy Spirit, we must remember the gifts of the Spirit are just that. They are gifts, not trophies. They are not ministry or identity builders. They are gifts of His grace, expressions of His love, and invitations to transformation. They are to build faith, hope and love in Jesus, not in the delivery boys and girls. They are His gifts to awaken hearts and glorify Him. We must maintain the value of operating in spiritual gifts without ever neglecting to follow the way of love (1 Corinthians 14:1).

Intimacy and Impact

As God works in us to reach the world through us, it is important that we live out of vibrant intimacy with Him, out of the sanctuary. When speaking of our ministry values, it is vital to remember that first and foremost we value our own relationship with Him. Anything we have to offer comes from Him; any lasting impact we have on the world around us will only come out of intimacy with God.

We aren't called to be spiritual recluses or trail blazing burnouts. Rather, we are to be friends of God who live a life of intimacy and impact as we simply do life with God in a naturally supernatural way. Partnering with Him to advance the kingdom flows out of our friendship with Him. Our prayer is that you will discover and live in the reality of God's love for you, embrace both intimacy and impact, and follow Him from the sanctuary to the streets.

Notes

[1]Wimber, John, and Kevin Springer. *Power Evangelism.* San Francisco: Harper Collins, 1986, page 19.

[2]Baum, L. Frank. *The Wonderful Wizard of Oz.* HarperCollins, 1900.

[3]Finley, James. *Merton's Palace of Nowhere: A Search for God through Awareness of the True Self.* Notre Dame, IN: Ave Maria Press, 1999, page 47.

[4]Mulholland, M. Robert, Jr. *Invitation to a Journey: A Road Map for Spiritual Formation.* Nottingham: IVP Books, 1993.

[5]Benner, David. *The Gift of Being Yourself.* Downers Grove, IL: InterVarsity Press, 2004, page 42-43.

[6]Williams, Don. Signs, *Wonders, and the Kingdom of God: A Biblical Guide for the Reluctant Skeptic.* Ventura, CA: Vine Books, 1989, page 108-109.

[7]Wimber, John, and Kevin Springer. *Power Healing.* San Francisco: Harper Collins, 1987, page 187-235.

[8]Manning, Brennan. *Ruthless Trust: The Ragamuffin's Path to God.* San Francisco: Harper Collins, 2000, page 5.

[9]Manning, Brennan. *Ruthless Trust: The Ragamuffin's Path to God.* San Francisco: Harper Collins, 2000, page 1.

[10] Boyd, Gregory. *Repenting of Religion.* Grand Rapids, MI: Barker Books, 2004, page 13-14.

About the Authors

Charles Bello (MBS) served as a senior pastor with the *Association of Vineyard Churches* for more than 25 years. He presently serves as a pastor to pastors, a spiritual director, educator, and the Director of *Pathways to Leadership*. He has spent the last 30 years ministering and training pastors, missionaries and lay leaders in more than 20 nations. He has authored, *Prayer as a Place* and *Recycled Spirituality*. He and his wife Dianna live in Edmond, Oklahoma and have six grown children and five grandchildren.

Brian Blount and his wife, Jeanine, have spent the last fifteen years equipping and training individuals, teams, and churches in healing, prophetic ministry, and power evangelism throughout Europe and the United States. He is a husband and the father of six children, the youngest three of which are triplets. He is a business owner of a graphics design company called Web Vision Graphics. He and his family currently live in Oklahoma City.

Other Books by Charles Bello

Prayer as a Place: Spirituality That Transforms

Prayer as a Place is an invitation to partner with Christ as he leads the believer into the dark places of his or her own heart. The purpose of this journey is to bring holiness and wholeness to the child of God. With candor and brutal honesty, Pastor Charles Bello shares his own reluctance and then resolve to follow Christ on this inward journey. In sharing his story, readers gain insight into what their own personal journeys may look like. *Prayer as a Place* reads like a road map as it explores the contemporary use of contemplative prayer as a means of following Christ inward.

Recycled Spirituality: Ancient Ways Made New

Recycled Spirituality is like browsing through a mysterious, ancient resale shop filled with treasures from the rich heritage of historical Christianity. Many of the ancient spiritual disciplines have continued to be in use for thousands of years—others are being newly rediscovered. These classical disciplines are drawn from our shared Catholic, Orthodox, Protestant, Evangelical and Pentecostal traditions.

Recycled Spirituality is written as a practical handbook to encourage and equip readers to push the borders of their own experience and personal faith traditions to encounter God in fresh ways. The purpose of these encounters is always transformation, renewal and missional living. As Charles writes, "The gift of tradition is meant to be received. The essence of tradition is meant to be rediscovered. And if the practice of a tradition helps form you into the image of Christ, it is meant to be recycled."

You can order these books and additional copies of *From the Sanctuary to the Streets* through www.coachingsaints.com. To contact Charles Bello or Brian Blount, go to www.coachingsaints.com